Aircraft of the
Royal Navy

Aircraft of the
Royal Navy

Paul Ellis

JANE'S

Copyright© Paul Ellis 1982

First published in the United Kingdom in 1982 by
Jane's Publishing Company Limited
238 City Road
London EC1V 2PU
ISBN 0 7106 0135 2

Designed by Bernard Crossland Associates

Printed in Great Britain by
Netherwood Dalton and Co Ltd, Huddersfield

For Buster

Introduction

Many hundreds of thousands of words have been written on the origins and history of the Royal Navy's Fleet Air Arm, and it is not within the scope of this book to tread again that familiar ground in any detail. Instead we will throw a small spotlight by the use of photographs onto a collection of aircraft which have made a particular contribution to aviation and, in some cases, world history.

Contained in the following pages are illustrated biographies of some 120 Royal Navy aircraft types, from the early fighters and reconnaissance biplanes used by the Royal Naval Air Service (RNAS) during the First World War to today's multi-mission Sea Harrier. Arranged chronologically, the collection embraces every conceivable maritime aviation role, from early attempts at fleet spotting to high-speed, low-level strike against enemy ships or shore-based targets, using the latest nuclear weapons. Also included are what many would regard as the backbone of the contemporary Fleet Air Arm, the anti-submarine helicopters which are the eyes and teeth of a naval task force.

To appreciate fully how naval aircraft have evolved over the past 60 or more years, and to understand why some lines of development have been pursued at the expense of other more promising avenues, it is worth looking briefly at how the Royal Navy's air arm itself has developed from the fledgeling Naval Wing of the Royal Flying Corps to the fully integrated Fleet Air Arm of today.

In the earliest days the Admiralty's interest in aviation centred on lighter-than-air machines, which their Lordships perceived as being most useful for "distant reconnaissance". The first of these, started in 1909, was the 500ft-long rigid airship *Mayfly*. This was not to be an auspicious start to British naval aviation, for the Vickers-built craft was wrecked within six months of delivery, in September 1911. Fortunately, the officers appointed to administer the *Mayfly*, Capt Murray Sueter and Cdr Oliver Schwann, were possessed of rather greater durability than their charge, and it is due in no small part to their great energies that naval aviation did not founder forever with the unhappy airship.

It should be understood that the Royal Navy was even then still experiencing the trauma of a number of sweeping reforms initiated by Admiral Fisher at the turn of the century, and there were many very senior officers within the Admiralty who were quite impervious to notions as revolutionary as the creation of a naval air arm. Having come to accept the dreadnought, they were understandably committed to a belief in the supremacy of big guns in naval warfare, a belief that would persist in some quarters right up to the outbreak of the Second World War.

In time, however, the wounds of the *Mayfly* debacle healed, and with the emphasis now on heavier-than-air machines, there began slow progress towards the creation of an establishment of aircraft and suitably trained personnel for the exclusive use of the naval staffs. Early pioneers, based at Eastchurch on the Isle of Sheppey, were Lts A. M. Longmore and C. R. Samson, of whom much more was to be heard. It was Samson who succeeded in making the first take-off from a ship, flying a Short S.27 from a platform erected over the fore-turret of the cruiser HMS *Africa* on January 10, 1912. Longmore, for his part, would become one of the first naval flying instructors before transferring permanently to the Royal Air Force and rising to become Air Chief Marshal Sir Arthur Longmore.

By the end of 1912 the Royal Flying Corps (RFC), consisting of separate naval and military wings, had been formed, and Murray Sueter was installed in the Admiralty as the first Director of the Air Department. By the end of the year the Naval Wing could muster 16 assorted aircraft and no fewer than 22 pilots.

The aeroplane in naval service was to remain essentially a reconnaissance tool for some years, although sporadic experiments in bomb and torpedo dropping were carried out. It was not until well into the First World War that there was anything resembling an actively offensive element of what on July 1, 1914, became the separate Royal Naval Air Service.

The rate of progress in the development of aircraft and weapons during the First World War was prodigious, as was the expansion of this new branch of the Navy. By the time it was once again merged with the RFC to form the Royal Air Force, on April 1, 1918, the RNAS had on strength almost 3,000 aircraft and 67,000 officers and men operating from 126 naval air stations around the world and from numerous surface ships.

During the war there began the gradual definition of the various uses to which naval aircraft could be put. These were, broadly, reconnaissance and spotting, conventional bombing of ships and shore-based targets, torpedo bombing of submarines and surface shipping, and interception of enemy aircraft and Zeppelins. All of these tasks could be performed by both seaplanes and land-based aircraft, the major difference between them being that, initially, only the seaplanes could operate from naval vessels at sea. All this changed in the latter part of the war when the first true aircraft carriers emerged, fitted with permanent flying-off decks capable of handling aircraft with conventional wheeled undercarriages.

With the coming of peace most of the impetus gained over the preceding four years was dissipated within a few months, and by the end of 1919 the naval branch of the RAF, as the RNAS had become, was reduced to a single spotter-reconnaissance squadron, one fighter flight, half a torpedo squadron, and single seaplane and flying-boat flights. There then followed 20 years of wrangling and bickering while the Admiralty attempted to regain control of its own air arm, an event which finally came to pass in May 1939.

In the meantime, success had to be measured in terms of numerous small concessions, usually won in the face of extreme opposition from hostile politicians and senior officers from other services. The first real breakthrough came in 1921 when it was agreed that henceforth only naval officers would fly as observers in naval aircraft. Subsequently it was agreed that 70 per cent of the pilots in what by then was called the Fleet Air Arm would be naval officers holding dual naval and RAF rank.

Money for the Fleet Air Arm was always limited, and the inter-war period was a time of stagnation. At the beginning of the period the Fleet Air Arm had only the carriers *Furious* and *Argus* in commission, the latter ship being the first with a fully flush deck suitable for operating the new generation of naval aircraft coming into service. Between 1922 and 1938, however, a further five carriers were commissioned: *Eagle* (1922), *Hermes* (1923), *Glorious* and *Courageous* (1928), and *Ark Royal* (1938). Progress in the development of new aircraft was slow, with most of the types emerging as biplane spotter-reconnaissance aircraft of unremarkable performance. But by September 1932 the strength of the Fleet Air Arm had risen to 26 flights, totalling 156 aircraft. In the following year the squadron superseded the flight as the basic carrier flying unit, and the existing six-aircraft flights were merged into squadrons of nine or twelve aircraft, with the exception of the small number of catapult flights embarked by cruisers and battleships. By May 1935 there were some 15 squadrons with a total of 175 aircraft, but at the outbreak of the Second World War in September 1939, by which time the Fleet Air Arm was once again totally under the aegis of the Royal Navy, there were still only 20 squadrons with 340 aircraft between them.

In all fairness, the Royal Air Force was hardly any better off in terms of the standard of aircraft foisted upon it by successive governments, and the types fielded by the two services frequently ran parallel: Fairey IIIFs in both the RAF and FAA; Fairey Gordons in the RAF complementing naval Fairey Seals; and Hawker Demons and Furies in the RAF counterparted by Ospreys and Nimrods in the Fleet Air Arm. Later the two services would share even more aircraft, including the Gladiator, Hurricane and Spitfire. In each case the Navy made what modifications it could to fit its aircraft for carrier flying. High on the list of vital developments at this time was the evolution of a safe method of recovering aircraft aboard the carrier. Early experiments with longitudinally laid arrester wires had been abandoned as being too costly in aircraft, and for a while naval aircraft were required to land with no artificial aids. By 1933, however, a system using transverse wires on the deck had been perfected on HMS *Courageous*, and from then on the tail-mounted arrester hook became standard on all carrierborne aircraft.

The greatest strides in naval aviation were undoubtedly made during the Second World War, both in terms of the aircraft operated by the Fleet Air Arm and also in the manner in which they were used. Senior officers quickly grew to appreciate the extraordinary advantages offered by seaborne air power, and for the first time British naval aircraft were used for decisive attacks on strategic and tactical targets, achieving a measure of success undreamt of during the First World War. Ranging far ahead of their parent carriers, they sought out and destroyed submarines, flew combat air patrols over invasion beaches and delivered crippling bomb and torpedo attacks against enemy surface shipping. Using a mixture of indigenous and American Lend-Lease aircraft, the Fleet Air Arm fought in every theatre, from the North Atlantic to the far South Pacific. At its zenith, in the middle of 1945, it had on strength about 3,700 first- and second-line aircraft, more than 70,000 personnel, 56 carriers of all types and some 56 RN shore establishments scattered all over the world. Compared with the underpowered and overweight biplanes of 1939, with maximum speeds seldom in excess of 150 mph, the latest strike fighters coming into service at the war's end flew at 400 mph or more and could deliver a ton of high-explosive over a range of more than 600 miles.

But with the coming of peace the familiar cycle of growth and collapse once more entered its violent downward trajectory. Within weeks of VJ-Day Lend-Lease escort carriers were streaming westwards, laden with surplus Hellcats, Corsairs and Avengers. By August 1946 the Fleet Air Arm had shed at least 59 front-line squadrons and a comparable number of second-line units.

Despite the wholesale pruning of aircraft and personnel there were compensations, for the end of the war also coincided with the beginning of jet aviation, and the Fleet Air Arm was in the forefront with experiments in the operation of this radically new type of aircraft. Among the most significant occurred in December 1945, when Lt Cdr E. M. Brown became the first pilot to land a purely jet-propelled aircraft on the deck of an aircraft carrier. The aircraft was a specially modified de Havilland Vampire, which he brought aboard the light fleet carrier HMS *Ocean*.

Other pioneering work during the 1950s added to Britain's high reputation as a leader in naval aviation, including the development of the steam catapult, which replaced the earlier hydraulic variety, the introduction of the angled flight deck and the invention of the mirror landing aid. Regretfully, these advances in carrier technology were not generally matched by improvements in the performance of Fleet Air Arm aircraft, and the Royal Navy began to slip astern of nations like the United States in both the quality and diversity of its shipborne aircraft.

Following the Korean War, during which RN aircraft, notably Fireflies and Sea Furies, had acquitted themselves particularly well, it soon became apparent that a powerful blue-water navy was an expensive and undesirable indulgence as the gradual withdrawal from territories abroad began. With this retrenchment came a determination to whittle down the armed forces to financially more manageable levels, and the Fleet Air Arm was among the first to suffer. The new generations of jet aircraft were proving extremely expensive to develop and deploy, and following an orgy of confused thinking that came to a climax with the 1966 Defence Estimates, the whole future of British naval air power seemed as bleak as in the dark days after *Mayfly*. Central to the 1966 policy was the cancellation of CVA-01, a new fleet carrier conceived in the early 1960s as the future backbone of the fixed-wing Fleet Air Arm. Henceforth, it was announced, the traditional roles of naval aircraft would be performed by shore-based aircraft of the Royal Air Force, a prospect which alarmed enlightened RAF officers no less than it did committed champions of independent naval air power.

In the event, matters were not destined to take quite so disastrous a turn, for in 1979 a new Conservative administration granted a stay of execution for the aircraft carrier, extending the life of HMS *Ark Royal* almost to the end of the 1970s. *Eagle*, however, went to the scrapyard.

That then should have been the end of the affair, with fixed-wing naval aviation the concern only of historians, and only helicopters carrying Royal Navy colours. But a marriage between a navalised version of the RAF's Harrier V/Stol strike fighter and a new concept in warships, originally called the "through-deck cruiser", was arranged in time to avert the demise of carrier flying in the Royal Navy. Although there are to be only 34 of these revolutionary aircraft embarked in just two (out of three ordered) *Invincible*-class carriers, the continuing need for a highly mobile air component within modern naval task forces should ensure that they remain in service through to the end of the 1990s.

Short 184, with torpedo slung between the main floats, is hoisted out over the Medway

Short Type 184 seaplane

The two-seat Type 184 was the Royal Navy's first practical torpedo-carrying aircraft and the prototype flew for the first time at Rochester early in 1915. Powered by a 225 hp Sunbeam engine, it was usually known by the RNAS as the "225," after the horsepower of its engine, while its more official designation was the serial number of the prototype, a common practice at that time.

Following the flight of a second prototype the Admiralty ordered an initial batch of ten aircraft. In addition to Short, no fewer than nine other

manufacturers received production contracts and more than 650 examples were eventually built. The first Short-built aircraft were delivered in mid-1915, with those from the subcontractors appearing towards the end of the year.

The privilege of carrying out the first operations went to the first and second prototype aircraft, which had embarked for the ill-fated Dardanelles campaign on board the converted Isle of Man packet HMS *Ben-my-Chree* in May 1915. On August 12 Flt Cdr C. H.

K. Edmonds made the first ever airborne torpedo attack, against a 5,000-ton Turkish supply ship off Injen Burnu. That this vessel was already aground following an attack by a British destroyer does not detract from the significance of Edmonds' feat.

Two other successful torpedo attacks were made during the campaign, but these were destined to be the last of this nature by the Allies during the First World War, mainly because of the Type 184's marginal performance when loaded with the 810lb Whitehead torpedo. Nevertheless, the groundwork

for future Fleet Air Arm expertise in torpedo warfare had been laid.

Nearer home, the Type 184 was more successful as a reconnaissance aircraft or light bomber. Replacing the 225 hp Sunbeam Mohawk engine with more powerful units, such as the 275 hp Sunbeam Maori III, resulted in progressively improved performance, but that did not tempt the Admiralty into re-introducing the torpedo as the aircraft's main armament. The Type 184 served to the end of the First World War and no fewer than 300 were still on charge in October 1918.

Although representative of some RNAS-operated machines, Avro 504 D7103 was actually an RFC aircraft

Avro 504

The Avro 504 is probably best remembered as a trainer, and in that role it was to remain in more or less continuous service with the Royal Air Force until the early 1930s. Countless pilots destined for both the RAF and the Fleet Air Arm in the inter-war years completed their initial flying training in A. V. Roe's frail-looking but in fact immensely strong two-bay biplane. But in the early stages of the First World War the 504 was one of a limited number of aircraft capable of front-line use

as a reconnaissance aircraft and bomber.

First flown in the summer of 1913 at Brooklands, it was adopted first by the RFC. The Admiralty received its first 504 a year later and by December 1914 Sqn Cdr Longmore's No 1 Squadron had six on strength.

Although "routine" bombing raids had been carried out by Wg Cdr Samson's Eastchurch Wing, based in Belgium, almost from the outbreak of war, the raid on the Zeppelin sheds at Friedrichshafen on November

21, 1914, by 504s did most to vindicate the Admiralty's policy of promoting the bomber aircraft.

RNAS Avro 504Bs, of which about 190 were built, with their characteristic long-span ailerons and large unbalanced rudder, were supplemented by about 80 504Cs, developed primarily for anti-Zeppelin operations. The 504E introduced the more powerful 100 hp Gnome Monosoupape and reverted to the more orthodox wing of the original 504,

although with reduced stagger, since the rear cockpit had been moved further aft to make room for a new fuel tank. Only ten were built and these found their way to the RNAS training schools at Chingford, Cranwell and Fairlop.

Final RNAS variant was the 504G, of which 30 were built. A gunnery training development of the 504B, it was fitted with a single fixed forward-firing (synchronised) Vickers machine gun and a Lewis gun mounted on a Scarff ring in the aft cockpit.

This Curtiss JN-3, No 1365, was delivered from the USA in March 1915

Curtiss JN series

The JN-3 was a two-bay biplane trainer which first flew in 1914. At that time the RNAS was in the throes of a massive build-up in strength and was in urgent need of a suitable elementary pilot trainer. An initial batch of six of these 90 hp Curtiss OX-5-powered aircraft was ordered for evaluation, and these were delivered in March 1915. Subsequently the Admiralty ordered a further 91, some 79 of which were built by the parent company in Hammondsport while the remaining 12 were completed by Curtiss (Canada) in Toronto.

The RNAS also acquired a number of similarly powered JN-4s for training. As many as 160 assorted JN-3s, JN-4s and JN-4As were later transferred to the RFC.

Sopwith Tabloid

For its day the diminutive Sopwith Tabloid, designed by T.O.M. Sopwith with F. Sigrist, was a most remarkable aeroplane. Built in 1913, it attained the astonishing speed of 92 mph in level flight, and with a passenger on board could climb to 1,200ft in one minute. Subsequent production Tabloids were single-seaters powered by the 100 hp Gnome Monosoupape rotary engine and with substantially the same performance.

It was ordered for both the RFC and the RNAS but in quite modest quantities compared with other scouts, less than 40 being built. First deliveries to the Navy were in the summer of 1914. The first operational success of any note came in October 1914 when two Tabloids (Nos 167 and 168) were despatched to attack the Zeppelin sheds at Cologne and Dusseldorf. The attack on Cologne was frustrated by bad weather but Dusseldorf was successfully attacked and Zeppelin Z.IX destroyed on the ground.

Tabloids were used by Wg Cdr Samson's Eastchurch Squadron in Belgium and also by No 3 Wing (as the Eastchurch Wing became) in the Dardanelles.

Armament consisted of a single 0.303in Lewis gun mounted on the wing centre-section or on the fuselage side, and a limited number of 20lb bombs (as used in the attack on the Dusseldorf Zeppelin shed) could also be carried.

An as yet un-numbered Tabloid at Brooklands

Caudron G.III and G.IV

The Caudron G.III, a development of the 1913 G.II, was a two-seat sesquiplane powered by an 80 hp Gnome or 100 hp Anzani engine. The G.III was originally used by French reconnaissance squadrons on the Western Front. The RNAS received a total of 124 and most of these were used for training, their tactical value having been assessed by the Navy as no more than marginal.

The G.IV twin-engined development of the G.III was used extensively by both the French Air Force and the RFC over the Western Front. In RNAS service it was used as a bomber and could carry up to 250lb of bombs.

The first RNAS unit to appreciate the potential of this aircraft as a bomber was Sqn Cdr Spenser Grey's No 5 Wing, based at Coudekerque in Belgium, in the spring of 1916. Notable successes were achieved against German seaplane, submarine and Zeppelin bases. Caudron G.IVs also operated with No 4 Wing at Petite Snythe (also in Belgium) under the command of Sqn Cdr C. L. Courteney.

A total of 55 G.IVs were delivered to the Royal Navy, 43 of them built by the French parent company and the other 12 by the British Caudron Co. The last of these curious-looking biplanes was phased out in the spring of 1917 following the arrival of the Handley Page O/100.

The Caudron G.II was similar in many respects to the G.III, which was operated by the RNAS during the early part of the First World War

Sopwith Schneider No 3734

Sopwith Baby with Le Prieur rockets on its interplane struts

Sopwith Schneider and Baby

The single-seat Schneider was a direct descendant of Harold Pixton's 1913 Schneider Trophy-winning Tabloid. Apart from the floats—two pontoons at the front and a third, smaller, float beneath the tail—there was little to distinguish the two aircraft. Performance of the Schneider was only marginally impaired by the extra drag of the floats, and the seaplane also weighed slightly more.

Production for the RNAS began in November 1914 with an initial order for 12 aircraft (Nos 1436 to 1447), all powered by the 100 hp Gnome Monosoupape rotary engine. Later refinements were the substitution of a larger, curved fin for the original triangular unit and the use of ailerons on both sets of wings in place of the old wing-warping arrangement. When production ended Sopwith had built 136 of these trim little aircraft, which were widely deployed amongst RNAS coastal stations as well as serving on board the Royal Navy seaplane carriers *Anne, Ark Royal, Ben-my-Chree, Campania, Empress, Engadine* and *Raven II.*

Armament consisted of a single Lewis gun firing upwards through an aperture in the top wing centre-section. A small bomb for use against U-boats could be carried below the fuselage, but there is no record of a successful attack with this weapon.

The Sopwith Baby had the same basic airframe as the Schneider, but mated to a more powerful 110 hp or 130 hp Clerget engine housed in an open-fronted horseshoe-shaped cowl.

The first batch of 100 Sopwith-built Babies (Nos 8118 to 8217) was delivered between September 1915 and the following July. The Baby was also built by Blackburn at Leeds, some 71 being completed with the 110 hp Clerget and a further 115 with the 130 hp engine.

Like the Schneider, Babies in RNAS service operated from seaplane carriers in the Mediterranean and North Sea and from numerous coastal stations, where they were primarily used for anti-Zeppelin patrols. Armament was one Lewis gun, either firing through the top wing centre-section in the manner of the Schneider, or placed above the nose and synchronised to fire through the propeller disc. Two 65lb bombs could also be carried, and on some aircraft the Lewis gun was replaced by Ranken darts, which were regarded as more suitable for attacking Zeppelins.

Curtiss H.4 Small America

The all-wood H.4 America reconnaissance flying boat was the first of several Curtiss designs to enter service with the RNAS, with the first pair (Nos 950 and 951) being acquired from British agents White and Thompson and delivered in November 1914. After trials at Felixstowe these boats were followed by additional production orders totalling some 62 aircraft, eight of which (Nos 1228-1235) were built in Britain.

The H.4s were not as successful as had been anticipated, with the 100 hp Anzani engines fitted at Felixstowe leaving them seriously underpowered. But they did enter operational service and were used for coastal patrols as well as more mundane training roles.

As with so many aircraft of that period, the H.4s were fitted with a variety of engines, with each fit necessitating a separate designation. When the larger and more powerful Curtiss H.12 appeared the H.4 Americas became known as Small Americas (the H.12s being, perforce, Large Americas). Armament consisted of flexibly mounted machine guns in the bows and a light bomb load whose size depended on the engines fitted. Typically, with 100 hp engines it was but twelve 20lb bombs or a pair of 100lb bombs.

Only three H.4s survived the war, the type having been declared obsolete for all purposes in August 1918. Their importance lies not so much in their fitness for fighting, which was limited, as in their contribution to the development of naval flying boat design, construction and operation.

Curtiss H.4 Small America No 3592

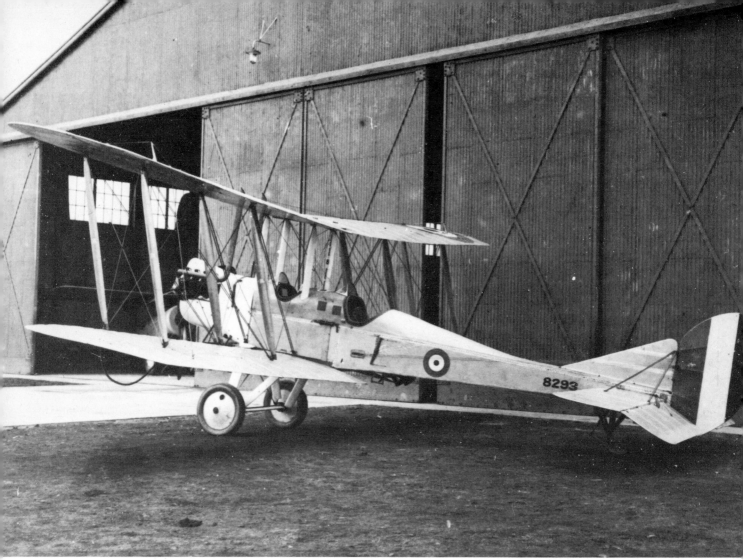

This BE.2A, No 8293, was built by the Grahame-White Co at Hendon

BE.2 series

Designed by the Royal Aircraft Factory, the two-seat BE.2C was a stable, lightly loaded two-bay biplane initially used by the RFC. It was not successful as a fighting scout, suffering appalling losses on the Western Front and precipitating the "Fokker Fodder" scandal. But with the RNAS, which used it as both a bomber and a patrol aircraft, it fared better, being deployed in generally less hazardous theatres of war.

The Admiralty ordered 337 BE.2Cs, about half of which were powered by the 70 hp Renault engine and half by the 90 hp RAF.1A. The type served with four operational units: No 1 Wing at Dunkirk, Nos 2 and 3 Wings in the Dardanelles and No 7 (Naval) Squadron in East Africa, as well as a number of

coastal air stations and training schools. British-based aircraft were generally used on anti-submarine and anti-Zeppelin patrols, in which they were not entirely unsuccessful.

Other, less important, BE types also served with the RNAS: the earlier BE.2A, the BE.2E and the BE.8 "Bloater".

The BE.2A served with the naval wing of the RFC from 1912, a total of only four aircraft being allocated to that branch of the service. The type served in Belgium with the Eastchurch Wing in 1914 and later in the Dardanelles.

The RNAS received about 95 BE.2Es from the RFC for training, and a handful of BE.8s for the same purpose.

Bristol Scout C and D

The original Bristol 206 Scout was designed by Frank Barnwell and first flew in February 1914. The Admiralty ordered 24 Scout Cs for the RNAS in November of that year (Nos 1243-1226) and these were built in parallel with 12 Scouts for the RFC. Some of the early RNAS aircraft were used on the Western Front and these were powered by the 80 hp Gnome rotary engine, which the Admiralty considered to be more reliable than the RFC's Le Rhône.

Most of the RNAS Scout Cs were used on anti-Zeppelin patrols from land stations at Chingford, Dover, Eastchurch, Great Yarmouth, Port Victoria and Redcar. Most carried no gun armament but could be armed with canisters of Ranken darts, which could be dropped on top of the hapless Zeppelins to set them on fire. It was a brave idea but not very successful and the long duration and high rate of climb of the big airships made them doubly difficult to catch and attack.

In an attempt to overcome this tactical disadvantage a number of Isle of Man steam packets had been converted into seaplane carriers, one of which, the former *Viking* renamed HMS *Vindex,* was equipped with a short flying-off deck. On November 3, 1915, Flt Sub-Lt H. F. Towler flew his Scout C from this deck, so making the first take-off from a ship by a wheeled aircraft.

By November 1915 Barnwell had developed the Scout D and the Admiralty ordered an initial batch of 50 (Nos 8951-9000). Most were powered by the 100 hp Gnome Monosoupape. Of the final batch of 30 aircraft (N5390-N5419), only the first ten had the Monosoupape, the remainder being fitted with the 80 hp Gnome.

No 8988 was a Bristol Scout D

Henri Farman

The two-seat Henri Farman pusher biplanes were amongst the first aircraft to be used operationally by the RNAS when war broke out in 1914. Produced in both landplane and seaplane form, the aircraft were built under subcontract by the Aircraft Manufacturing Co at Hendon and were used for reconnaissance, bombing and training.

Originally powered by a 80 hp Gnome rotary engine, the aircraft had a performance which was, by any standard, only marginal. With two crew, fuel for three hours' flying and such rudimentary armament as the occupants cared to take with them, the Farman was often hard-pressed to leave the ground. Later, re-engined with the 140 hp Canton Unné, the

Farman was used as a light bomber. This version was designated the F.27 and was an altogether larger aircraft with a primary structure of steel tubing.

Farmans served in several theatres during the First World War, notably the Dardanelles. When the Eastchurch Wing left Belgium for the Eastern Mediterranean it numbered among its meagre company eight early Farmans. These are recorded as having been the least useful of the Wing's aircraft.

In the Dardanelles Wg Cdr Samson was lucky enough to get some of the F.27 version, and it was from one of these that, in December 1915, he succeeded in dropping a 500lb bomb on a Turkish barracks.

This un-numbered aircraft is an early Henri Farman

The RNAS used several versions of the single-seat Nieuport Scout, including the Type 11, seen here in French markings

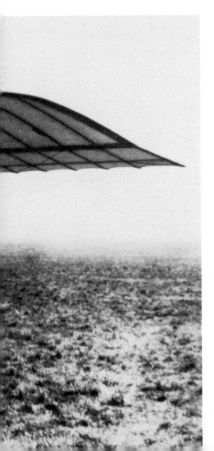

Nieuport scouts

The RNAS used a number of single-seat Nieuport scout types during the First World War, the first of which was the Nieuport 11. Six of these small biplanes, with their characteristic Vee interplane struts, were delivered to Wg Cdr Samson's No 3 Wing in the Dardanelles in July 1915.

On the Western Front the RNAS used both the Nieuport 17, powered by the 110 hp Le Rhône, and the larger Nieuport 24 with a 120 hp engine.

The Nieuports were great fighting aircraft and from mid-1916 to 1917, when they were replaced by Sopwith Pups and Triplanes, the Scouts were used for all manner of defensive and offensive operations, serving with no fewer than eight naval squadrons. Most were armed with a Lewis gun mounted above the wing centre-section, or a synchronised Vickers placed above the engine cowling. Some aircraft had Le Prieur rockets on their interplane struts for use against German kite balloons.

Flight of Short Bombers in Belgium

Short Bomber

The Bomber was a longer-span landplane version of the Type 184 seaplane. Produced to meet an Admiralty requirement of 1915 for a long-range bomber capable of carrying heavy loads over long distances, the prototype, No 3706, was a conversion of the Type 184 with transposed crew positions within a re-worked fuselage and new two-bay wings developed from those of the Short Type 166 seaplane.

The definitive aircraft, however, had an extra 6ft bay inserted in each side of the wing assembly to improve load-carrying capability. Lack of stability in pitch and yaw resulted in the fuselage also being lengthened. This was done in the face of initial opposition from Horace Short, who was concerned that structural problems might result.

Production contracts were awarded to Short (36 aircraft) and, under subcontracts, to the Sunbeam Motor Car Co at Wolverhampton (15 aircraft), Mann, Egerton & Co at Norwich (20), Parnall & Sons, Bristol (six)

and The Phoenix Dynamo Co of Bradford (six). Not all of these contracts were fulfilled, however, with a total of only 55 aircraft being completed.

First operational unit to receive its Bombers was No 7 (Naval) Squadron at Coudekerque, which went into action on November 15, 1916, with an attack on the submarine pens at Zeebrugge. This unit continued to carry out modest bombing raids throughout the winter of 1916-17. Also equipped was No 3 Wing at Luxeuil, which received 15

Bombers. From this unit eventually sprang the Independent Force, RAF, forerunner of Bomber Command.

A request from the RFC for bombing aircraft eventually led to some 14 aircraft being transferred from the RNAS in addition to one new Phoenix-built example.

Few if any RNAS Bombers survived the war, the type having been superseded by more advanced designs such as the Handley Page O/100.

Short 827/830

Short Brothers at Rochester produced a bewildering variety of seaplanes to Admiralty order both before and during the First World War. Among them were the S.41, Admiralty No 42, the Admiralty Type 74, the Type 135 and the Type 166 seaplane.

The Type 827, which followed on from the Type 166 seaplane, was powered by a 150 hp Sunbeam Nubian in-line engine,

while the Type 830 had a 140 hp Salmson water-cooled radial similar to that used in the Type 166.

The first contract, placed in mid-1914, was for six Type 827s (Nos 822-827) and six Type 830s (Nos 819-921 and 828-830). When production eventually ended more than 100 Type 827s had been completed, against only 18 or so Type 830s.

Following satisfactory trials from the seaplane carrier HMS *Campania* during June 1915, the Type 827 entered quantity production at Short and a number of subcontractors, including Brush Engineering of Loughborough, Fairey at Hayes, Parnall and the Sunbeam Motor Car Co at Wolverhampton.

The Type 827 was widely

deployed amongst a number of RNAS coastal stations from 1915, including the Isle of Grain, Calshot, Dundee, Killingholme and Great Yarmouth. Intended for both anti-submarine and anti-Zeppelin patrols as well as for training, they were armed with a single free-mounted Lewis gun and carried racks below the fuselage for light bombs.

Short 827 at Rochester

No 1335 was a Short Type 830

This Nieuport 12 Two-Seater was built in Britain by William Beardmore

Nieuport 12 of No 2 Wing RNAS, based in the Dardanelles in 1916

Nieuport Type 12 Two-Seater

Generally known as the Nieuport Two-Seater, the Type 12 entered service with both the RFC and the RNAS during 1915 and was used for reconnaissance and light bombing. Slightly larger than the Nieuports 11 and 17, the Two-Seater was powered by either a 110 hp or 130 hp Clerget engine, and the pilot and observer sat in tandem. Nieuport 12s used by No 3 Wing in the Dardanelles were normally flown solo, armed with a single Lewis gun mounted above the top wing centre-section.

The first batches of Two-Seaters for the RNAS were built by Nieuport at Issy-Les-Moulineaux but 50 aircraft (Nos 9201-9250) were later built in Britain by Beardmore at Dalmuir. In all, some 194 were acquired by the RNAS.

In addition to Wg Cdr Samson's No 3 Wing in the Dardanelles, No 2 Wing at Dunkirk and Imbros and No 1 Wing, also at Dunkirk, used the Nieuport 12.

Wight Converted Seaplane

This two-seat three-bay biplane, built by J. Samuel White & Co on the Isle of Wight, was produced to supplement RNAS Short Type 184 seaplanes. Adapted from the land-based Wight Bomber (N501), which never entered quantity production, the Converted Seaplane was built during 1917.

From a total of 50 ordered only 37 were completed, most being powered by the 250 hp Rolls-Royce Eagle. Primary role for the aircraft was anti-submarine patrol, and four 100lb or 112lb bombs could be carried. A Wight seaplane from the RNAS station at Cherbourg was responsible for the first sinking of an enemy submarine in the English Channel, on August 18, 1917.

When the war ended in November 1918 only a handful were still operational and these were quickly declared obsolete.

Wight Converted Seaplane No 9853

No 9063 was a Norman Thompson NT.4A

Norman Thompson
NT.2 and NT.4

The NT.2B, built by the Norman Thompson Flight Company of Bognor Regis, Sussex, was a two-seat dual-control flying-boat trainer which was used by the RNAS at Calshot, Felixstowe and Lee-on-Solent. It was a development of the 1914 White and Thompson No 3 Boat.

A number of engines were fitted to this aircraft, amongst them the 150 hp or 200 hp Hispano-Suiza, 200 hp Wolseley and 200 hp Sunbeam. Early aircraft had the 160 hp Beardmore. Although a relatively large number were ordered and built, many were kept in store awaiting engines and were not used operationally by the Royal Navy. In addition to Norman Thompson, S. E. Saunders Ltd at Cowes and Supermarine Aviation Works at Woolston, Southampton, also built NT.2B airframes.

The NT.4 four-seat anti-submarine aircraft was the first design to be built after the old White and Thompson company changed its name to Norman Thompson in October 1915. Powered by a pair of 200 hp Hispano-Suiza engines, it resembled the Curtiss H.4 Small America, one of the principal differences being that on the NT.4 the propellers were arranged as pushers rather than tractors.

Repeated problems with the engines led to the cancellation of production contracts after only 31 aircraft had been built, and all had been withdrawn from service by the end of the war.

22

Sopwith 1½-Strutter

The 1½-Strutter was the Royal Navy's first truly useful two-seat scout fighter. The prototype was completed in December 1915 and carried the official designation of Sopwith Type 9400. The popular name derived from the arrangement of the interplane and cabane struts.

The first production examples of this conventional fabric-and-wood aircraft appeared in February 1916 and the first RNAS unit to operate the type, No 5 Wing at Coudekerque, Belgium, received its aircraft in April that year. This unit's 1½-Strutters were first used for escorting the Wing's Breguet and Caudron bombers but later they were employed to good effect as bombers in their own right against German batteries and other major targets.

Sopwith 1½-Strutter at Brooklands during 1916

S.90   SOPWITH 1½ STRUTTER. 2 SEATER FIGHTER.   110 HP

DESIGNED & BUILT BY
THE SOPWITH AVIATION & ENGINEERING C? L?

Sopwith 1½-Strutter just after take-off from HMS *Argus*

A single-seat bomber variant, designated Sopwith Type 9700, was also produced. In this aircraft the rear cockpit was eliminated to provide internal stowage for four 65lb bombs. The bombers were earmarked for No 3 Wing, based at Luxeuil.

The Royal Navy received a large number of 1½-Strutters: about 420 of 550 ordered were two-seaters, the remaining 130 being the single-seat bomber variant.

As the war drew to a close and the 1½-Strutter began to be outclassed on the Western Front by the new generation of fighting scouts, the type entered a new phase of service as a shipboard scout. A great deal of development work on operating aircraft from carrier decks was performed by RNAS 1½-Strutters fitted with both wheeled and skid undercarriages. The first successful landing using deck arrester gear was made on board HMS *Argus* by Wg Cdr Bell-Davies in October 1918.

25

Morane-Saulnier Type L

The two-seat Type L was unusual in that it was a parasol-wing aircraft. Although it seemed impossibly frail and singularly underpowered, with an 80 hp Le Rhône rotary engine, it was remarkably successful in its time.

First of a long line of monoplane fighters produced by the brothers Morane and their partner Raymond Saulnier, the Type L first flew in 1913. On the outbreak of war it was ordered in large quantities by the French Army. The RNAS first ordered the type at the end of 1914 and a total of 25 were delivered (Nos 3239-3263).

Although they carried no standard armament, RNAS Parasols were fitted in the field with rudimentary racks to carry up to six 20lb bombs. It was with an aircraft thus armed that Flt Sub-Lt Warneford of No 1 (Naval) Squadron won his VC for the first destruction of a Zeppelin by an aircraft in the air. This feat occurred over Bruges on June 7, 1915, when Warneford, flying Morane No 3253, succeeded in dropping his six bombs on LZ.37, which subsequently exploded and crashed in flames. Unhappily Warneford was killed just ten days later during a flight over Paris in a Henri Farman.

Apart from Warneford's success the Parasol did not have a particularly distinguished career with the RNAS, although French Army aircraft enjoyed better fortune.

Morane-Saulnier Type L of No 1 Wing, RNAS, at Imbros in 1915

The strange PB.25 with swept-back upper wing

Pemberton-Billing PB.25

This single-seat pusher biplane fighter was a direct development of Noel Pemberton-Billing's PB.23E, built in 1915. Later in the following year the Admiralty ordered 20 examples (Nos 9001-9020) of a modified version for the RNAS.

The first PB.25 was powered by a 110 hp Clerget engine driving a two-bladed propeller, but the remainder of the production batch were all powered by the 100 hp Gnome Monosoupape driving four-bladed propellers. All had been delivered by February 1917 (though at least six were without engines) and the type operated briefly from the RNAS stations at Eastchurch and Hendon. Handling qualities were said to be unpleasant and unpredictable and the performance was generally agreed to be lamentable. Armament consisted of a single 0.303in Lewis machine gun mounted in the nacelle in front of the pilot.

The RNAS abandoned the PB.25 in favour of the new Sopwith aircraft then entering service during the course of 1917, and surviving aircraft were scrapped.

This DH.6, C7887, was built by the Grahame-White Co at Hendon

de Havilland DH.6

The two-seat DH.6 was not a particularly inspiring aircraft, either to look at or, by all accounts, to fly. It collected more than its fair share of epithets, amongst them "The Crab," "Clutching Hand," "Flying Coffin" and, from Australia, "Dung Hunter".

Originally conceived as a two-seat elementary trainer for use by the Royal Flying Corps, the type flew for the first time in 1916. Airco and several subcontractors then set to and between them built no fewer than 2,000.

The DH.6 did not see widespread service in the RNAS until the end of 1917, when more than 300 were transferred from the RFC for use on anti-submarine patrols around the coast of Britain. Some 34 RNAS DH.6 flights were formed, five of which were manned by US Navy aviators based in North-east Ireland.

The aircraft achieved no notable successes with the RNAS and only one attack, an abortive attempt to sink UC-49 in May 1918, is recorded. At the end of the war the Admiralty was quick to divest itself of the type and all surviving DH.6s had left the service by early 1919.

29

Sopwith Pup No 9918

Sopwith Pup

The single-seat Pup was a conventional single-bay biplane powered by an 80 hp Le Rhône rotary engine. It was a delightful aircraft to fly, with sensitive, well harmonised controls, and its low wing loading allowed it to maintain a height advantage better than any of its contemporaries on either side.

Officially designated Sopwith Type 9901, the Pup flew for the first time in February 1916 and entered service with No 1 Wing on the Western Front. The celebrated No 8 (Naval) Squadron, commanded by Sqn Cdr G. R. Bromet, was equipped with the type and, operating from Vert Galand, supported RFC units from October 1916 until the following February, when it was relieved by No 3 (Naval) Squadron, also flying Pups.

Apart from serving with

distinction on the Western Front, RNAS Pups were also involved in more nautical tasks, such as patrols and escort duties in support of naval units. They were also used extensively in the development of deck-flying operations by landplanes. The Pup will always be associated with the experiments carried out by Sqn Cdr E. H. Dunning, the first man ever to land an aircraft on the deck of an aircraft carrier, who alighted on HMS *Furious* on August 2, 1917.

Experiments like this led to the aircraft being deployed on board a number of aircraft carriers, including *Argus*, *Campania* and *Manxman,* in addition to *Furious*. Pups were also launched from flying-off platforms on the cruisers *Caledon, Cassandra, Cordelia, Dublin, Repulse* and *Yarmouth.*

Sopwith Triplane N5438

A brand-new Pup, less serial, awaiting delivery

Sopwith Triplane

Unusual in configuration but light and highly manoeuvrable, the Triplane was one of the outstanding fighting scouts of the First World War. Although ordered initially for the RFC it was used exclusively by the RNAS on the Western Front, where it was flown by Nos 1, 8, 9, 10 and 12 (Naval) Squadrons.

The Triplane's design owed a great deal to its predecessor the Pup, having a similar fuselage and tail, but with three narrow-chord wings arranged with equal gap. Powered by a 110 hp Clerget rotary engine, the prototype, N500, was flown for the first time at Brooklands by Harry Hawker on May 30, 1916. As testament to the new aircraft's handling and sound structure, he is said to have looped the little triplane three minutes after take-off. Armed with a single Vickers gun, N500 carried out its service trials with "A" Squadron RNAS at Furnes aerodrome in June. The type then entered service with Nos 1 and 8 (Naval) Squadrons in February 1917 and with No 10 Squadron in May that year.

By November, however, the Triplane had largely been supplanted by the Camel. But during its brief career it succeeded in destroying a large number of German aircraft. Most notable were the victories of the five "Black" fighters of Naval 10's "B" Flight, which despatched no fewer than 87 assorted enemy aircraft between May and July 1917.

Total production appears to have been some 152 aircraft, including four prototypes and a further four aircraft built for the French Government but subsequently returned.

Handley Page O/100

The twin-engined O/100 landplane bomber was Handley Page's classic reply to Commodore Murray Sueter's equally classic request for a "bloody paralyser" of an aeroplane to help in holding back the German advance on Antwerp in the early stages of the First World War.

The original specification was for a large patrol bomber designated Type O and with a wing span of 114ft. This was issued in December 1914 as the basis of a contract for four prototypes powered by a pair of 150 hp Sunbeam engines and capable of carrying up to six 100lb bombs.

The need for a practical wing-folding system to permit the aircraft to be hangared reduced the wing span to 100ft (although compensation for this piece of surgery was available in the form of more powerful engines), and the design henceforth became the Type O/100. The eventual prototype contract, awarded in February 1915, covered four Rolls-Royce Eagle-engined aircraft (Nos 1455-1458) with substantially increased bomb load.

The first prototype (1455), with enclosed cabin for the crew, was completed at Cricklewood in November 1915 and was transported by road to Hendon, where it flew for the first time on December 18. In the following January it was ferried by Sqn Cdr Longmore to Eastchurch, where the enclosed cockpit was removed. On the second prototype the nose was converted to a long, open structure accommodating the two pilots side by side and the nose gunner ahead of them, and this arrangement was retained for all subsequent production aircraft.

Deliveries to the RNAS began in the summer of 1916 and the first unit to be equipped, starting in August, was the "Handley Page Squadron," which was assigned to the 3rd Wing at Luxeuil-les-Bains. With the disbandment of No 3 Wing in June 1917 its two O/100s (1459 and 1460) joined No 5 Wing at Coudekerque, whence they made frequent daylight raids against the U-boat pens at Bruges, Zeebrugge and Ostend, and against German long-range shore batteries.

The first RNAS unit to operate the aircraft in strength, however, was No 7 Squadron, whose speciality became night bombing raids against a whole catalogue of strategic targets.

While almost all of the RNAS O/100s were based either in Britain or on the Continent, one aircraft (3124) did find its way to Mudros in the Aegean, where it bombed, amongst other targets,

the city of Constantinople. This
aircraft was eventually lost in
the Sea of Xeros, near Sulva
Bay, although its crew survived
to be taken prisoner.
Total production for the RNAS
amounted to 46, almost all of
them being powered by
Rolls-Royce Eagle engines. Six
were experimentally fitted with
Sunbeam Cossack engines but
they were not used
operationally.

Handley Page O/100

Short 320 photographed in 1916

Short 320 seaplane

The Type 320 was designed to meet a requirement for a long-range seaplane capable of delivering the 18in Mk IX torpedo and was the last of a long line of Short seaplanes to enter service with the RNAS during the First World War.

Designated Type 320 because of its 320 hp Sunbeam Cossack engine, it flew for the first time in 1916. A production contract for 30 aircraft was awarded in January 1917 and the first 12 were ferried to No 6 Wing at Otranto in time to commence operations in September of that year with an abortive attack against submarines lying off Cattaro in the Adriatic.

No further torpedo attacks were made with the Type 320 and thereafter the torpedo crutch was replaced by racks designed to carry two 230lb bombs.

In all, 127 were built, the majority by Short but also two batches by Sunbeam. At the time of the Armistice there were still about 50 in service.

AD Flying Boat No 1520 was built by Pemberton-Billing Ltd

AD Flying Boat

The AD Flying Boat was a
two-seat patrol and
reconnaissance aircraft
designed by the Air Department
of the Admiralty to Specification
N.2A and built by
Pemberton-Billing (later to
become Supermarine).
Construction of two prototypes
(Nos 1412 and 1413) was
completed during 1916 but
essential hull modifications
delayed flight tests until early
1917.

The two prototypes were
followed by 27 production
aircraft powered by either a 150
hp or 200 hp Hispano-Suiza or a
200 hp Wolseley Python engine.
The first production aircraft was
tested at the Isle of Grain in
September 1917 and at least

four were still there when the
war ended in November 1918.
Of the remainder, 17 are
reported as having been
delivered to store direct from
production, while four others
were either wrecked in test
flights or deliberately tested to
destruction.

The AD was not successful in
RNAS service. It was difficult to
handle both in water
manoeuvres and during
take-off, and the French-built
geared Hispano engines gave
persistent trouble. It is worth
noting, however, that a number
of hulls were repurchased by
Supermarine after the war and
modified for passenger-carrying
as the Supermarine Channel.

This RNAS 1F.1 Camel excites the curiosity of French troops somewhere on the Western Front

Sopwith Camel

There can be few people with even a cursory acquaintance with the history of aviation who have not heard of the Sopwith Camel. In most minds it is exclusively linked with the exploits of the Royal Flying Corps on the Western Front, but of the 1,300-odd enemy aircraft destroyed by the type during the First World War almost 400 fell to the guns of RNAS Camels.

The Royal Navy used two versions of the Camel: the F.1 single-seat fighting scout powered by a 130 hp Clerget or 150 hp Bentley BR.1 engine, and the similarly powered 2F.1 Camel, which was specifically designed as a shipboard aircraft.

The first RNAS F.1 Camels entered service on the Western Front in July 1917 and by later that summer three squadrons were equipped with Clerget-engined aircraft. Later the Bentley-engined Camels began to appear in strength and

RNAS Sopwith Camel

most of the earlier aircraft were re-engined.

The shipboard 2F.1 Camel differed in several respects from the land-based aircraft. More use was made of steel in the construction to cut down on corrosion, and the entire rear half of the fuselage could be detached aft of the cockpit to increase storability on board ship.

First flown in March 1917, the shipboard Camels were used extensively on anti-Zeppelin patrols over the North Sea and were flown off numerous battlecruisers and light cruisers as well as from the aircraft carrier HMS *Furious.*

In all, some 150 were built under subcontract by Beardmore, and contracts for more than 130 additional aircraft were cancelled. By war's end there were almost 130 still in service, 112 of which were embarked in ships of the Grand Fleet.

Fairey Hamble Baby

That the diminutive Hamble Baby appeared to owe so much of its outward appearance to the house of Sopwith was no accident, for it was based to a large extent on the Sopwith Baby. Nevertheless, the Fairey Company invested a great deal of its own expertise in the aircraft, not least the Fairey patent camber-changing gear (the forerunner of today's trailing-edge wing flaps).

The Hamble Baby was produced by Fairey at Hayes and Hamble and, under subcontract, by Parnall & Sons at Bristol. Most Hamble Babies were in fact built by Parnall—130 against Fairey's 50—and they could be distinguished by their retention of Sopwith-style fins and rudders and, in the case of the seaplane version, of Sopwith floats. Most of the 74 Parnall Hamble Baby landplane conversions were used at the various RNAS training establishments.

Most of the Babies, powered by 110 hp or 130 hp Clerget rotary engines, were used on anti-submarine patrol from RNAS coastal stations at Calshot, Cattewater and Fishguard. Abroad they were stationed at Santa Maria di Leuca in Italy, Suda Bay on the island of Crete, Syra, Talikna and Skyros in the Aegean, and Port Said and Alexandria in Egypt. Two Hamble Babies, together with four Sopwith Babies, flew from the seaplane carrier HMS *Empress*.

Hamble Babies were operational during 1917 and 1918, but with the end of the First World War they were rapidly withdrawn from service to make way for more modern types.

American-built Curtiss H.12B N4332

Parnall-built Fairey Hamble Baby

Curtiss H.12 Large America

The H.12 Large America was a twin-tractor biplane flying boat carrying a crew of four. Generally regarded as the most famous of the First World War flying boats, it was developed from the H.4 Small America and served with the RNAS from the spring of 1917 until after the war ended in November 1918.

Large Americas were particularly valuable on anti-submarine and anti-Zeppelin patrols and succeeded in destroying a modest but useful number of each of these antagonists. A Great Yarmouth-based aircraft, No 8666, shot down Zeppelin L.22 on May 14, 1917, while No 8677 destroyed L.43 exactly one month later. Submarine successes were UC.36, sunk on May 20, 1917, and UB.20,

claimed on July 29 that year.

A total of 50 H.12s (Nos 8650-8699) and 21 H.12Bs (N4330-N4350) were delivered to the RNAS; all were American-built. The H.12s were delivered with 160 hp Curtiss engines, but these units were found to leave the aircraft seriously underpowered and were replaced by 275 hp Rolls-Royce Eagles. The H.12Bs, also Rolls-Royce-powered, incorporated minor modifications. All Large Americas suffered from weakness of the hull planing bottom and arrangements were made for the hulls to be strengthened in Britain. Aircraft thus modified were known as Large America Converts.

At the end of the war some 18 H.12s, six of which were Converts, were still in service.

Sopwith T.1 Cuckoo N6954

Sopwith Cuckoo

The T.1 Cuckoo was a single-seat carrierborne/shore-based torpedo-carrier, the Royal Navy's first ever aircraft in that category. Previous torpedo-carriers, like the Short 184, had been seaplanes and had little in the way of performance, particularly in sea states above flat calm.

Sopwith was invited to consider a landplane torpedo-carrier in late 1916 by Commodore Murray Sueter. The prototype Sopwith T.1, N74, first flew in June 1917 powered by a 100 hp Hispano-Suiza engine; later production aircraft had the 200 hp Sunbeam Arab.

Tests were carried out at the Isle of Grain during the following month and an order for 100 T.1s was confirmed on August 16, the aircraft to be built by the Fairfield Shipbuilding and Engineering Co Ltd of Glasgow.

In February 1918 the Blackburn Aeroplane & Motor Co received an order for 230 T.1s, while Pegler & Co at Doncaster was awarded a contract for 50. First of the subcontracted aircraft to be completed came from Blackburn in May 1918, but with the Armistice production orders were drastically cut and the total number delivered to the Navy was 212.

The type first entered service at East Fortune with the Torpedo Aeroplane School and first embarked in HMS *Argus* in October 1918, operating alongside Sopwith Camel 2F.1s and Short 184s.

After the First World War the Cuckoo, as the T.1 had by then been named, served on the aircraft carriers *Furious* and *Eagle* and was also used for development work on torpedo warfare at HMS *Vernon,* the shore establishment at Gosport housing the Royal Navy's torpedo school. The Cuckoo was eventually declared obsolete for all purposes in 1923, when No 210 Squadron at Gosport was disbanded.

Felixstowe flying boats

The Felixstowe series of long-range flying boats was the result of work done by Sqn Cdr John Porte on improving the Curtiss H.4 Small America and the H.12 Large America.

The Felixstowe F.1 was a hybrid aircraft comprising the wings and tail of an H.4 mounted on a new hull of Porte's own design and with the 100 hp Anzani engines of the Curtiss replaced by a pair of 150 hp Hispanos.

Four H.4 airframes—Nos 950, 1230, 3545 and 3569—were used initially in Porte's experiments, culminating in the total modification of No 3580. Built at Felixstowe, this new hull was known as the Porte 1, with the completed aircraft being designated Felixstowe F.1.

The new Porte hull was markedly superior to that of the standard Curtiss, and a larger version was produced to utilise the wings and tail of the H.12 Large America. Known as the F.2, the aircraft, serialled 8650, was powered by two 250 hp Rolls-Royce engines. Trials were successful and quantity production of the type was authorised.

The production aircraft, now powered by two 345 hp Rolls-Royce Eagle VIII engines, were designated F.2As and a

total of almost 100 were completed by the end of the First World War.

The F.2As operated from a number of coastal flying-boat stations around Britain on long-range anti-submarine and anti-Zeppelin patrols. Armament consisted of two 230lb bombs and up to five Lewis guns. In order to make the aircraft more visible in the event of a forced landing in the sea (not a rare occurrence, it seems), the F.2As were in the latter

stages of the war painted in distinctive and unique patterns and colours.

Operating from the RNAS coastal stations at Calshot, Dundee, Felixstowe, Great Yarmouth, Killingholme, Scapa Flow and Tresco, the F.2A boats gave valuable service, particularly in 1917, when the U-boat war was at its height.

The Felixstowe F.3 was a larger development of the F.2A and was capable of carrying a

larger load over a longer range. Despite these apparent advantages, however, the F.3, powered by two 345 hp Rolls-Royce Eagle VIIIs, was less manoeuvrable and consequently less well equipped to take on enemy seaplanes in the way that the more compact F.2As had. Nevertheless, more than 260 were ordered, of which just over 100 had been completed before the end of the war caused a general cancelling of contracts.

Fairey Campania aboard its parent ship, the *Campania*

N6101 was an SB.3F variant with folding undercarriage

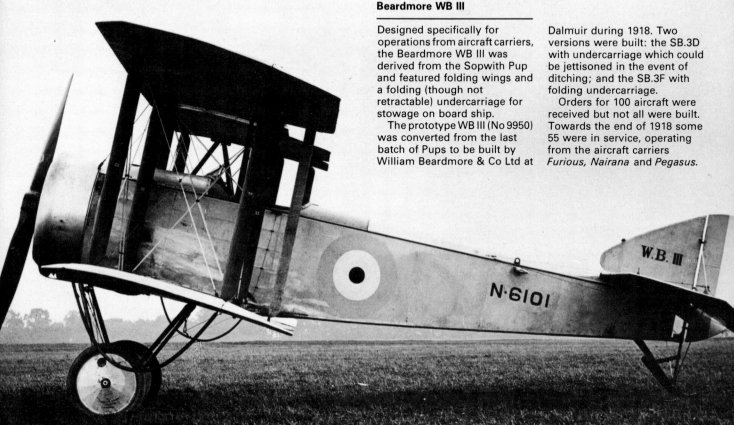

Beardmore WB III

Designed specifically for operations from aircraft carriers, the Beardmore WB III was derived from the Sopwith Pup and featured folding wings and a folding (though not retractable) undercarriage for stowage on board ship.

The prototype WB III (No 9950) was converted from the last batch of Pups to be built by William Beardmore & Co Ltd at Dalmuir during 1918. Two versions were built: the SB.3D with undercarriage which could be jettisoned in the event of ditching; and the SB.3F with folding undercarriage.

Orders for 100 aircraft were received but not all were built. Towards the end of 1918 some 55 were in service, operating from the aircraft carriers *Furious*, *Nairana* and *Pegasus*.

Fairey Campania

The Fairey Campania was a two-seat, two-bay biplane powered by a 275 hp Sunbeam Maori II or 345 hp Rolls-Royce Eagle VIII. Designed in 1916, it was the first aircraft to be built specifically for operation from an aircraft carrier, and the aircraft's name derived from its carrier vessel, the former Cunard liner *Campania.*

Of 100 Campanias contracted for, only 62 were completed, 50 by the parent company at Hayes and 12 by subcontractor Barclay Curle & Co of Glasgow. The prototype, powered by a 250 hp Rolls-Royce Eagle IV, flew for the first time on February 16, 1917.

Apart from shipborne service aboard *Campania* the seaplanes also operated from RNAS stations at Bembridge, Calshot, Cherbourg, Dundee, Newhaven, Portland, Rosyth and Scapa Flow. No spectacular operational successes were attributed to the type and the Campania was declared obsolete in August 1919.

Fairey IIIA, B and C

The Fairey III series was a development of the N.9 and N.10 experimental seaplanes built in 1917. The N.9, a single-bay biplane powered by a 200 hp Rolls-Royce Falcon I engine, first flew in July 1917. The N.10, a larger and heavier two-bay aircraft powered by the 260 hp Sunbeam Maori II engine, flew for the first time on September 14, 1917.

N.10 was fitted out as a landplane before being bought back by Fairey, and in this configuration it was the subject of an Admiralty order for 50 aircraft, to be designated Fairey IIIA. Intended as a successor to the Sopwith 1½-Strutter, the IIIA came too late to make any contribution to the war effort and was declared obsolete in 1919.

The IIIB was a seaplane derivative of the IIIA and some 25 were built, a small number of which entered service at RNAS coastal stations before the end of the war. Powered by a Sunbeam Maori II engine, it flew for the first time on August 8, 1918.

Last and most famous of the trio of early operational Fairey biplanes was the IIIC. Designed as a two-seat general-purpose seaplane, it arrived too late to be used operationally during the war. It was a true hybrid of the two earlier machines, combining the equal-span two-bay wings of the IIIA with the float undercarriage of the IIIB. Power was provided by the 375 hp Rolls-Royce Eagle VIII. A total of 36 were produced from September 1918, the first six production machines being converted from IIIBs already on the line.

First unit to receive the IIIC was No 229 Squadron at RNAS Great Yarmouth. The type also saw limited action during 1919 while operating from HMS *Pegasus* as part of the North Russian Expeditionary Force.

Fairey IIIA N2851 on wheels

Curtiss H.16 Large America

The H.16 Large America was a considerable advance over the earlier H.12 boat and incorporated many of the lessons learned, particularly with regard to hull strength.

Initially some 15 were ordered (N4060-N4074), powered by two 250 hp Rolls-Royce Eagle engines, and the first was delivered in early 1918. A contract for an additional 110 was awarded but with the end of the war in November the last 50 were cancelled.

The H.16s were late entering service because tests at the Isle of Grain with N4060 revealed that the aircraft was tail-heavy, and further trials resulted in a long list of modifications. These included altering the step of the planing hull, installing a second pilot's seat with associated dual controls, altering the tailplane incidence and fitting balanced ailerons.

When the end of the war came only about 15 were operational, most being held in store at Norwich, Brockworth and Sherburn.

Float-equipped Fairey IIIC

de Havilland DH.9

The two-seat, two-bay DH.9 was intended as a longer-range replacement for the DH.4. Despite being modelled closely on and even having some major components in common with its predecessor, it was not destined to enjoy anything like the DH.4's success. To be fair, the cause was not so much the airframe as the Siddeley-built BHP and Puma engines, which left the DH.9 seriously underpowered.

First flown in July 1917, it entered squadron service in early 1918. Three RNAS bombing squadrons in Belgium—Nos 2, 6, and 11 (Naval) Squadrons—were equipped. With the formation of the Independent RAF in April 1918 these squadrons were renumbered Nos 202, 206 and 211 Squadrons RAF.

In addition to limited bombing operations, RNAS aircraft were used for anti-Zeppelin and anti-submarine patrols from coastal stations (Great Yarmouth, Mullion, Padstow and Durgh Castle), and on naval co-operation work from a number of Mediterranean and Aegean bases.

After the war most DH.9s were declared obsolete, though a handful survived to be used for deck-landing trials on the aircraft carrier HMS *Eagle* in 1921.

DH.9 D2789

Parnall Panther

The Panther two-seat carrierborne spotter-reconnaissance biplane is significant in Fleet Air Arm history in being one of the first British aircraft to be designed specifically for carrier operations.

Designed by Harold Bolas to Admiralty Specification N.2A, the prototype first flew in 1917, powered by a 230 hp Bentley BR.2 engine. Initially the Admiralty ordered 300 Panthers, but with the signing of the Armistice in November 1918 this figure was cut to 150 aircraft. All were built by Bristol at Filton during 1919 and 1920.

These unattractive aircraft incorporated some novel features to suit them to their naval task. To conserve space when embarked the fuselage was made to fold just aft of the rear cockpit, the entire rear fuselage and tail assembly swinging to starboard. Both cockpits were set particularly high on the fuselage, which required the pilot to gain entry through a hole cut in the top wing. A hydrovane placed ahead of the wheeled undercarriage was designed to prevent the aircraft from nosing over in the event of a forced landing in the sea.

Four fleet spotter flights were equipped with the Panther and embarked on the carriers *Argus* and *Hermes.* At first carrier operations were hazardous in the extreme, the result of an arrester system which combined longitudinal deck wires with hooks placed on the aircraft's undercarriage axle. Nevertheless, the Panther remained in front-line service with the Fleet Air Arm until 1926, when it was replaced by the Fairey IIID.

Parnall Panther N7423, built by British & Colonial Aerc (later the Bristol Aeroplane Co)

N9500 was the prototype Westland Walrus

Westland Walrus

The Walrus was a three-seat carrierborne spotter-reconnaissance aircraft which flew for the first time in 1920. A two-bay biplane powered by a single 459 hp Napier Lion II engine, it was the result of an Air Ministry attempt to save money by modifying the de Havilland DH.9A for carrier operations.

The conversions were carried out by Westland at Yeovil and involved altering the fuselage to accommodate a third crew member, substantially reducing the stagger on the wings, and adding naval equipment such as flotation bags and arrester gear.

The type first entered squadron service in 1921. Total production amounted to only 36 aircraft, which served with No 3 Squadron (RAF) at Leuchars and Nos 420 and 421 Flights at Gosport. The last Walruses were withdrawn at the end of 1925 when 420 Flight re-equipped with Blackburn Blackburns and 421 Flight with Avro Bisons.

This Nieuport Nighthawk, H8539, was later converted to Mars X standard

Nieuport Nightjar

The Nightjar single-seat carrierborne fighter saw brief operational use between 1922 and 1924.

A total of just 22 were produced, and they were conversions of the RAF's Nighthawk by the Gloucestershire Aircraft Company (later Gloster) at Sunningend. Essentially the same as the Nighthawk, the naval aircraft were modified by fitting a special wide-track and longer-stroke undercarriage with special "jaws" on the axle casing to engage the fore-and-aft arrester wires then in use on Royal Navy aircraft carriers. Powerplant was the 230 hp Bentley BR.2 rotary engine and armament consisted of a pair of 0.303in Vickers machine guns on the front fuselage top.

The Nightjar entered service with No 203 Squadron at Leuchars in July 1922, replacing the unit's Sopwith Camels. Six airframes were ferried to the Middle East on board HMS *Argus* in September 1922 for operations during the Chanak crisis in Turkey. The type also served with 401 Flight until replaced by the Fairey Flycatcher in March 1924. It was not a particularly successful aircraft, however, and there were a number of fatal accidents, usually during the final landing approach, when the aircraft had a tendency to flick suddenly and spin in.

Avro Bison

The Fleet Air Arm has had more than its fair share of ugly aircraft during its lifetime, but few have equalled the grotesque Bison for lack of aesthetic appeal.

Designed as a fleet spotter to Specification 3/21, the Bison was, despite its unlovely aspect, both a practical and useful aeroplane with a large internal cabin to accommodate all the paraphernalia of naval observers of the day.

The prototype Avro 555 Bison I, N153, flew for the first time in 1921, powered by a water-cooled 450 hp Napier Lion engine. Twelve production Bisons were built, the first entering service with No 3 Squadron RAF at Gosport in 1922. First naval unit to be equipped was No 423 Fleet Spotter Flight, also based at Gosport, which later took its aircraft to sea on board HMS *Eagle*. The Bison also operated from HMS *Furious* with the Home Fleet. All had been superseded by the Fairey IIIF by 1929.

The main production variant was the Bison II, some 41 of which were built to Specification 16/23. This differed from the Bison I in having a raised centre-section, large dorsal fin and a two-bladed propeller replacing the Bison I's four-bladed unit.

Avro Bison I N155 with original flush top wing and small tail fin

Bison II N9848 displays the definitive raised top wing and the large fin extension

N9708 was one of a batch of seven Parnall Plovers

Parnall Plover

The Plover was a single-seat single-bay biplane designed to meet Air Ministry Specification 6/22 for a deck-landing fighter to succeed the Nieuport Nightjar. This was the specification so ably met by the Fairey Flycatcher.

Designed by Harold Bolas and built by George Parnall & Co at Bristol, the first two prototypes of the all-wood Plover were powered by the 436 hp Bristol Jupiter engine, while the third had the 385 hp Armstrong Siddeley Jaguar; production aircraft were fitted with the Jupiter.

Only ten production Plovers were built, mainly because of the FAA's adoption of the Flycatcher as its principal fleet fighter, and these served with Nos 403 and 404 Fleet Fighter Flights. All were replaced during 1924.

Fairey Flycatcher N9905. Note the "jaws" on the undercarriage axle, designed to catch the longitudinal arrester wires

Fairey Flycatcher

The Flycatcher was probably one of the first Fleet Air Arm aircraft to truly capture the popular imagination. And it achieved this as much by the widespread enthusiasm of its pilots as by its comparative ubiquity and longevity. Built to Air Ministry Specification 6/22, which called for a single-seat fleet fighter to replace the Nieuport Nightjar, it was powered by an uncowled 400 hp Armstrong Siddeley Jaguar.

In appearance the Flycatcher fell somewhere between the elegant and the offensive, with its angular fin and rudder assembly, awkward undercarriage and the strangely cocked fuselage profile. In plan, however, the rounded wing and tailplane tips and perfect symmetry lent it a gracefulness that photographers occasionally captured.

The first prototype Flycatcher flew for the first time from Hamble on November 28, 1922, in landplane form. The second prototype was a floatplane and flew for the first time in the following May, while the third was flown as an amphibian. This last configuration was not particularly successful and was not widely used.

Total production between 1923 and 1930 amounted to 195 aircraft. The type was destined to remain the standard fleet fighter from 1923 until 1934, and the Fleet Air Arm's only aircraft of that type between 1924 and 1932.

The Flycatcher was widely deployed during its career, serving with at least nine front-line flights and squadrons at sea as well as with land-based training squadrons. All of the fleet carriers of the day embarked the type at one time or another.

Flycatcher N9928 overflies HMS *Eagle*

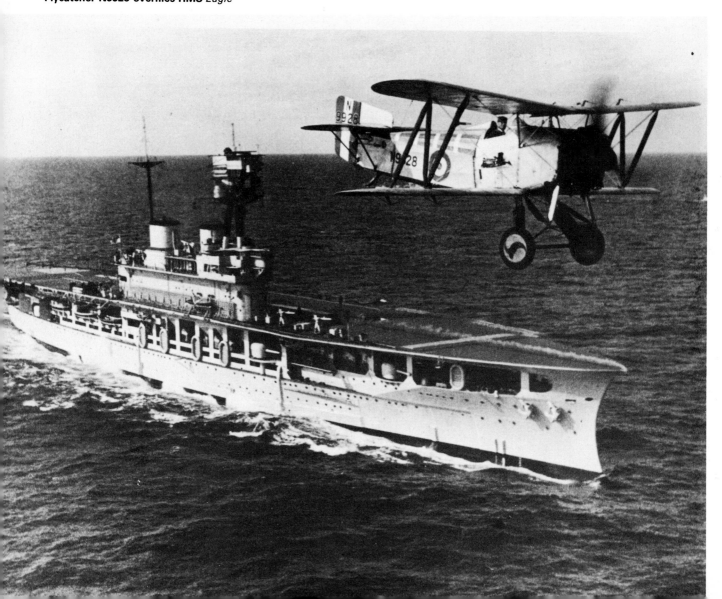

Flycatchers of No 405 Flight over Grand Harbour, Valetta, Malta

Blackburn Dart

This single-seat carrierborne torpedo bomber was a direct development of the T.1 Swift, which first flew in the summer of 1920. Powered by the 450 hp Napier Lion, the Swift underwent development test flying during the rest of 1920 and the first half of 1921. However, no production contract was forthcoming from the Air Ministry, which opted instead for a modified version to Specification 3/20 with shortened wings and powered by the Napier Lion.

The first production Darts appeared in 1921 and after deck-landing trials and performance measurements at Martlesham Heath two of the three prototypes, N141 and N142, were handed over to the development squadron in March and May 1922 respectively.

A production contract for 26 aircraft was awarded after competitive trials with three Handley Page HP.19 Henleys, and deliveries commenced in March 1922. The Dart soon established a reputation as a safe and pleasant aircraft to take to the deck, and the type was to remain in service for some ten years, enabling the FAA to develop its expertise in torpedo warfare to a high level.

Further contracts followed, and by the time production ended in 1928 no fewer than 117 had been built. The Dart served with many units during its career, flying from the carriers *Eagle*, *Furious* and *Courageous*. Amongst its many contributions to the art and science of carrier flying was the first night deck landing, on HMS *Furious* in July 1926.

Blackburn Dart N9629

The pilot of this ditched Dart, N9811, patiently awaits rescue

Supermarine Seagull III

Supermarine Seagull III photographed in 1923

The Seagull III was a three-seat carrier-based amphibian flying boat intended for spotter-reconnaissance duties. An all-wood aircraft of conventional appearance, it was powered by a single 450 hp Napier Lion X engine.

The definitive production aircraft was developed from the prototype Supermarine Seal of 1921 and the Seagull I and Seagull II of 1922. Initial production amounted to only eight aircraft, excluding the prototype, with deliveries commencing in 1923.

Only one Fleet Air Arm unit was equipped with the type: No 440 (Fleet Reconnaissance) Flight, based on board the aircraft carrier HMS *Eagle,* which was attached at that time to the Mediterranean Fleet. This unit received six Seagull IIIs but they remained active for only two years, No 440 Flight re-equipping with Fairey IIIDs in 1925. The Seagulls were then transferred to land-based duties with the RAF on Malta, where they remained until replaced by Fairey IIIF seaplanes in 1928.

Fairey IIID Mk II S1019 over Malta

Fairey IIID

The three-seat Fairey IIID was a natural successor to the IIIC and was to appear as both a seaplane and a landplane, powered by the 375 hp Rolls-Royce Eagle VIII or the 450 hp Napier Lion.

The IIID flew for the first time in August 1920 as a seaplane. The first production batch of 50 aircraft, ordered to Specification 38/22, were all powered by Eagle engines. All subsequent naval aircraft, less one small batch of six aircraft, were all fitted with Napier Lions of one mark or another. In all, some 207 IIIDs were built between 1924 and 1926.

The first Fleet Air Arm units to receive their IIIDs were Nos 441 and 444 Flights, in 1924. No 441 Flight's aircraft were landplanes and replaced Parnall Panthers. Operating initially from the carrier HMS *Argus,* the aircraft were equipped with axle-mounted hooks designed to engage the ship's fore-and-aft arrester wires. This system was not without its hazards, however, and in 1926 it was decided to dispense with landing aids altogether.

In addition to Nos 441 and 444, at least five other flights were equipped with the type, and the IIID was embarked on *Hermes, Tamar, Furious* and *Vindictive* in addition to *Argus.*

Blackburn Blackburn

Designed by Major F. A. Bumpus to Specification 3/21, the Blackburn R.1 Blackburn was a contemporary of the Avro Bison and shared that aircraft's complete lack of fineness of line.

The Blackburn, a two-bay biplane with a generous cabin for the observer, was powered by a 450 hp Napier Lion engine. Three prototypes were built during 1922 at the Olympia Works, and these were flown at Brough by R. W. Kenworthy before handling tests at A&AEE Martlesham Heath in July and August of that year.

The first naval unit to be equipped, in 1923, was No 422 (Fleet Reconnaissance) Flight, embarked on HMS *Eagle* with

Blackburn Blackburn I S1049: not a pretty sight

the Mediterranean Fleet and
also operating from Hal Far on
Malta. Blackburns also
equipped Nos 420, 449 and 450
Flights, flying from the carriers
Furious, *Eagle*, *Argus* and
Courageous.

A total of 33 Mk Is were built
between 1922 and 1924, with a
further 29 Mk IIs being built
between 1925 and 1926 to
Specification 11/23. These
differed from the Mk I in having a
raised mainplane
centre-section, cleaned-up
undercarriage and no
wing-mounted fuel tanks.

Two Blackburns were
converted to dual-control
trainers and unofficially named
Blackburn Bull. The widened
front fuselage created
prodigious drag, and the Bull's
marginal performance can be
gauged from a rate of climb that
barely exceeded 100ft/min.
The Blackburn Blackburn was
finally declared obsolete in early
1933, having been replaced by
the markedly superior Fairey
IIIF.

Fairey IIIF

The elegant IIIF was the last in
the line of Fairey III biplanes. It
was built in larger quantities
than any of its predecessors: a
total of 622 were completed, of
which 350 served with the Fleet
Air Arm.
Designed initially to
Specification 19/24, the IIIF was a
three-seat
spotter-reconnaissance aircraft
powered by the 570 hp Napier
Lion XIA. The prototype was
flown for the first time by
Norman Macmillan on March
19, 1926. Although a
development of the IIID, the
metal-structured IIIF was an
altogether more refined aircraft
with much better performance.
The first of the production Mk I
aircraft, of composite
wood-and-metal construction,
was flown initially in February
1927. Powered by the Lion VA
engine, it was followed by the
Mk II fitted with the Lion XI. In
the IIIF Mk III the wooden wings

of the Mks I and II were replaced
by a new all-metal structure.

The IIIF entered service first
with the RAF, in 1927, the Fleet
Air Arm not being equipped with
the first of its aircraft until the
following year, when No 440
Flight relinquished its IIIDs. Over
the next four years IIIFs replaced
the Avro Bisons, Blackburn
Blackburns and Blackburn
Ripons of some ten Fleet Air
Arm flights.

Later, when the FAA flights
had been merged or
redesignated as squadrons, the
IIIF was to equip no fewer than
five spotter-reconnaissance
squadrons: Nos 820, 822, 823,
824 and 825. Having operated
from every one of the Royal
Navy's aircraft carriers at some
time, the IIIF was generally
withdrawn during 1936
although not finally declared
obsolete until 1940.

Fairey IIIF Mk II S1253

The float-equipped S1521 was a IIIF Mk IIIB

Parnall Peto N255 overflies the ill-fated submarine *M.2*

Parnall Peto

Although not destined to serve in quantity with the Fleet Air Arm, the two-seat Peto biplane is worthy of note as one of only a handful of aircraft designed to operate from submarines. In the case of the Peto the carrier was the *M.2*, built by Vickers and commissioned in 1919. She was commissioned as a carrier in 1927 and was equipped with a hangar and catapult on her forward deck.

The Peto itself was designed by Harold Bolas to Specification 16/24. Two prototypes were built, N181 and N182; an apparent third machine which appeared in 1926 serialled N255 was in fact a rebuild of N181.

It was a compact twin-float aircraft with foldable wings braced by Warren-girder interplane struts. Although constructed largely of wood, the Peto was designed with many stainless steel fittings in an effort to eliminate corrosion.

First flown in the early spring of 1925, it was originally powered by the 135 hp Bristol Lucifer IV engine. Later this was supplanted by an Armstrong Siddeley Mongoose of the same power.

The Peto did operate briefly from *M.2* but the combination was not particularly successful. *M.2* was lost off Weymouth in January 1932 and it is believed that the inadvertent opening of the hangar doors was responsible.

A Peto is swung outboard by a crane mounted above the capacious hangar of *M.2*

The experimental Ripon II, N231, with torpedo visible beneath the fuselage

Ripon II S1564 of 462 Flight was later converted to Baffin standard

Formation of torpedo-armed Ripon IIs

Blackburn Ripon

Another design by Major F. A. Bumpus, the Blackburn T.5 Ripon was to be the Fleet Air Arm's standard carrierborne torpedo bomber during the early 1930s, succeeding the Blackburn Dart.

Designed to Air Ministry Specification 21/33, the prototype flew for the first time on April 17, 1926, powered by a 570 hp Napier Lion. The initial production version was designated Ripon II and differed from the prototype in having a cleanly cowled engine with the radiator removed to a position aft of the engine. The vertical tail and undercarriage were also substantially modified.

Production contracts for 20 Mk IIs were placed during 1928-29, followed in 1930 by contracts for 40 Mk IIAs to Specification 2/29. The Mk IIA was followed in 1931-32 by 31 production Ripon IICs with increased sweepback on the wings and modified wing construction.

Ripons replaced Darts in Nos 460, 461 and 462 Flights and formed the initial equipment of Nos 465 and 466 Flights, which embarked in HMS *Furious* during 1931. In 1933 these flights were reformed as Nos 810, 811 and 812 (Fleet Torpedo Bomber) Squadrons. From January 1934 the Ripon was gradually replaced by the Baffin.

Hawker Nimrod

The single-seat Nimrod was a carrierborne counterpart to the RAF's Fury fighter and was produced to replace the Fleet Air Arm's well loved Fairey Flycatchers, which had been in service since 1924.

Although externally similar to the Fury, the naval aircraft followed a distinct and separate line of development which effectively started with Specification N.21/26 issued in 1926. Successful trials with the private-venture Hoopoe—which, although not designed specifically to N.21/26, was nevertheless evaluated for that purpose—encouraged Hawker to continue development not only of the radial-engined Hoopoe but also of a Kestrel-powered version, around which was later drafted Specification N.16/30.

Originally known as the Norn,

the prototype, carrying the company registration HN.1, flew early in 1930 powered by a Rolls-Royce F.XIMS engine. This aircraft, together with a second machine for ground test, was taken on Air Ministry charge under the new name Nimrod.

A production order for 35 aircraft was placed in 1931 and the first of these, S1577, flew for the first time on October 14 that year. Trials with this aircraft were carried out at Martlesham Heath; the second prototype, S1578, was fitted with twin floats and evaluated at Felixstowe.

The first production Nimrod Is, which were not fitted with deck arrester gear, were delivered to No 408 Flight on HMS *Glorious* during 1932, followed by No 402 Flight on the *Eagle*. In 1933 the Fleet Air Arm

was reorganised, resulting in the merging of various shipboard flights. Nimrod units thereafter were 800 Squadron aboard HMS *Courageous*, 801 Squadron aboard *Furious* and 802 Squadron in *Glorious*.

The Nimrod II, to Specification N.11/33, incorporated arrester gear, swept-back upper and lower wings, enlarged tail surfaces, and the new Rolls-Royce Kestrel V. Production began in September 1933 and a total of 36 were built, three of them with an experimental stainless steel primary structure.

Nimrods continued to serve with the Fleet Air Arm almost until the outbreak of the Second World War, the last of 802 Squadron's aircraft aboard *Glorious* having been replaced by Sea Gladiators in May 1939.

Mixed bag of Nimrods and Ospreys

Nimrod II K5056

Nimrods of 800 Squadron over HMS *Courageous*

Hawker Osprey

The Osprey was related to the Royal Air Force's Hart as the Fleet Air Arm's Nimrod was to the Fury. It was the Navy's first two-seat carrierborne fighter-reconnaissance type and served continuously until declared obsolete for all purposes in 1940.

In 1926 Specification O.22/26 called for a high-performance fleet spotter-reconnaissance aircraft with a secondary capability as an interceptor. In addition, the aircraft was to be suitable for both wheeled and seaplane operations. No suitable design was forthcoming at first, and the Fleet Air Arm had to wait for the appearance of the RAF's Hart, the prototype of which, J9052, was adapted to meet the requirements of O.22/26 and first flown in its new guise in the summer of 1930.

Other contenders also emerged, from Fairey, Blackburn and Short Brothers, but Hawker's Osprey won the production contracts.

Two prototypes, S1677 and S1678, were followed by 37 production Osprey Mk Is powered by the Rolls-Royce Kestrel II. Together with the single-seat Nimrods they began to replace the Fleet's Fairey Flycatchers aboard the carriers HMS *Eagle* and *Courageous* from 1932, while float-equipped aircraft were issued to the 2nd Cruiser Squadron of the Home Fleet.

The Mk Is were followed into production by 14 Mk IIs and 49 Mk IIIs, the last-named equipped with a dinghy (in the starboard upper wing) and a Fairey Reed metal propeller.

Final production variant for the Fleet Air Arm was the Osprey Mk IV powered by the Kestrel V. Only 26 were produced, during 1935, and most of these served as floatplanes with the 3rd Cruiser Squadron in the Mediterranean and Middle East. Some wheeled aircraft served with 800 Squadron in HMS *Courageous,* 801 in *Furious* and 802 in *Glorious* as replacements for earlier marks lost in the normal course of carrier flying.

No 803 Squadron (the former 405 Flight), which since 1933 had been embarked in both *Eagle* and *Hermes,* was the last unit to use carrierborne Ospreys. After transferring its aircraft to *Ark Royal* during 1938, No 803 replaced them with Skuas the following year.

Withdrawn from front-line use, Ospreys were used for target-tug duties and for advanced flying training until finally declared obsolete in 1940.

Ospreys of No 407 Flight, which served with the 2nd Cruiser Squadron of the Home Fleet

Fairey Seal

Originally known as the Fairey IIIF Mk VI, the Seal was built to Specification 12/29 and, like its predecessor, was a three-seat spotter-reconnaissance aircraft. Powered by a 525 hp Armstrong Siddeley Panther IIA engine, it first flew as a landplane on September 11, 1930, and as a seaplane in September 1932.

Production aircraft featured a revised, rounded fin and rudder assembly and a tailwheel in place of the skid used on the IIIF. Following an initial batch of 11 aircraft production eventually totalled 91.

First deliveries were made in 1933, to Nos 820 and 821 Squadrons embarked in HMS *Courageous*. During the following three years Nos 822, 823 and 824 Squadrons were re-equipped with the type. By 1938, however, the Seal had been replaced in front-line squadrons by the Fairey Swordfish, although it was to continue in second-line use until the outbreak of the Second World War in 1939.

Fairey Seals of 824 Squadron

Walrus I K8552

Vickers-Supermarine Walrus

The Walrus was a single-engined biplane spotter-reconnaissance amphibian which carried a crew of three. Designed by R. J. Mitchell and developed as a private venture under the name Seagull V, the prototype, K4797, flew for the first time on June 21, 1933, powered by a 635 hp Bristol Pegasus II radial engine.

First production order, for 24 machines, was placed by Australia in 1933, but the Fleet Air Arm did not order the aircraft until May 1935, following evaluation by No 702 Catapult Flight aboard the battleship HMS *Nelson*.

The initial production contract for the Fleet Air Arm was to Specification 2/35 and covered 12 Walrus Is. Following yet more trials, orders for an additional 204 aircraft were placed, to Specification 37/36, the aircraft to be employed as the standard fleet spotter type on all catapult-equipped ships of the Royal Navy.

A total of 287 Walrus Is were built by Supermarine before production was transferred to Saunders-Roe. This Isle of Wight-based company built a further 453 Walrus IIs before all production ended in January 1944. Saunders-Roe aircraft differed from Supermarine-built examples in having a wooden as opposed to metal hull and in being powered by the 775 hp Pegasus VI engine in place of the Walrus I's IIM2.

The Walrus I entered service with the Fleet Air Arm in the summer of 1936, serving on board battleships and cruisers. In January 1940 the type constituted the major part of the equipment of No 700 Squadron, the parent unit of all catapult flights aboard Royal Navy warships. The Walrus also served with Nos 701, 710, 711, 712 and 714 Squadrons.

From 1941 the Walrus was also extensively used by the RAF on air-sea rescue missions. From 1944 the type was gradually replaced in FAA service by the Sea Otter, although some remained with the naval air-sea rescue unit, No 1700 Squadron, until as late as June 1946.

Blackburn Baffin

The Blackburn B-5 Baffin was little more than a Ripon with a 565 hp Bristol Pegasus radial engine in place of the earlier aircraft's water-cooled powerplant. Choice of the new engine was largely dictated by the resulting saving in weight, which could be exploited as increased payload.

Two prototypes, initially known as Ripon Vs, were built at Brough during 1932, one with the two-row Armstrong Siddeley Tiger and the other with the single-row Pegasus. The latter version was chosen to be the production aircraft and Air Ministry Specification 4/33 was written around it. A production order for 29 Baffin Is was placed in late 1933 and the first of these entered service with 812 Squadron in January 1934. Both 810 and 811 Squadrons subsequently re-equipped with the type. The last production aircraft was delivered in June 1935.

In addition to aircraft built to Baffin standard from scratch, a number (as many as 68) of Ripons were converted into Baffins over a period of two years.

The Baffin offered performance only marginally better than that of the Ripon and the type was finally declared obsolete in September 1937 after the three front-line squadrons had re-equipped, 811 and 812 Squadrons with the Fairey Swordfish and 810 with the Blackburn Shark.

K3589, an early production Baffin

Baffin K4071 of 810 Squadron

Baffin K3589 awaits delivery to the Fleet Air Arm

Blackburn Shark

The two/three-seat torpedo-spotter-reconnaissance Shark originated in the private-venture Blackburn B-6, or T.S.R., which was built to Air Ministry Specification S.15/33. The B-6 flew for the first time on August 24, 1933, and, powered by the 760 hp Armstrong Siddeley Tiger VI engine, could be flown as either a landplane or a seaplane.

The first production contract, for 16 aircraft, was placed in August 1934 and the type entered service with No 820 Squadron at Gosport in May the following year. The Shark I was followed into production by the Shark II, a total of 126 of which were built during 1935 and 1936. Two more front-line squadrons were equipped—No 810, embarked on HMS *Courageous,* and 821 on board *Furious*—as well as six training units at Lee-on-Solent, Worthy Down and Eastleigh.

Final and largest production contract was for 95 Shark IIIs, placed in January to Specification S.19/36. These were all delivered between April and December 1937 and differed from earlier aircraft in having a glazed sliding cockpit canopy and three-bladed wooden propeller.

Front-line service life was relatively short, for by 1938 Nos 820, 821 and 822 Squadrons had re-equipped with the Fairey Swordfish, their Sharks having been reassigned to such second-line duties as target-towing and the training of naval observers and telegraphists. Nevertheless, some Sharks remained operational, albeit in second-line units, until as late as 1944, when they were in use at Piarco, Trinidad.

Front of Shark I K4349, showing the torpedo mounting

K4295 was the prototype B-6, later converted to Shark II standard

Fairey Swordfish

The Swordfish biplane torpedo bomber symbolises more than any other naval aircraft of the Second World War the spirit and heroic achievement of the Fleet Air Arm. Obsolete, or at best obsolescent, when war broke out, it succeeded in transcending the British tradition of providing its armed forces with the least effective compromise available at the time. In doing so the Swordfish showed itself to be under many conditions an ideal fighting aircraft, even when faced by some of the best weapons the Axis could hurl against it.

Universally and affectionately known as the "Stringbag," the Swordfish originated from a succession of biplane prototypes that included the G.4/31 with its cowled Armstrong Siddeley Tiger engine, and the S.9/30 and TSR.I designs. The S.9/30 had an

in-line Rolls-Royce Kestrel and the TSR.I a Bristol Pegasus in a Townend ring, later to become a familiar sight on the Swordfish itself.

The private-venture TSR.I was destroyed in a spinning accident in September 1933, but the Fairey team had been sufficiently encouraged by other aspects of its handling and performance to produce a version designed to meet Specification S.15/33 for an advanced torpedo-spotter-reconnaissance aircraft. This aircraft, designated TSR.II (K4190), was slightly larger than the TSR.I and, powered by a 690 hp Bristol Pegasus IIIM3 radial engine, flew for the first time on April 17, 1934.

After protracted tests at Martlesham Heath the type was accepted for service and the name Swordfish adopted. In

early summer 1935 the Air Ministry placed an order for three pre-production and 86 production examples. The first of the pre-production aircraft, K5660, flew for the first time on December 31, 1935. Further contracts followed rapidly and by 1940, when Swordfish production was switched to Blackburn, the parent company had delivered no fewer than 692 aircraft.

Blackburn built a total of 1,700, consisting of 300 Mk Is, 1,080 Mk IIs and 320 Mk IIIs. The initial batches of Mk IIs retained the Pegasus IIIM3 engine but later aircraft had the Pegasus XXX. In addition, the Mk II featured a strengthened lower wing for carrying rocket projectiles. The Mk III, which, like the Mk II, first appeared in 1943, incorporated ASV Mk XI radar housed in a radome between the undercarriage legs.

K5660, the first pre-production Swordfish, during trials

K5660 just after dropping her "fish"

Fairey-built Swordfish I L2728

Its low landing speed made the Swordfish a popular aircraft with even the most inexperienced pilots

Swordfish first reached Fleet Air Arm squadrons in July 1936, when 825 Squadron relinquished its Fairey Seals. This unit was still embarked in HMS *Glorious*, cruising in the Indian Ocean, when the war began. By the end of that year both Nos 811 and 812 Squadrons had exchanged their Baffins and 823 Squadron its Seals for the new aircraft. By the time that 810, 820 and 821 Squadrons had been similarly re-equipped, the inimitable Stringbag had become the FAA's sole torpedo bomber type and would remain so until early 1940, when the first Albacore appeared.

The varied and widespread exploits of this extraordinary aircraft during the Second World War cannot be described here in anything more than the most cursory way. A total of 25 front-line Swordfish squadrons were formed, together with a further 22 second-line squadrons and 11 catapult flights, each of which would make its own contribution to the navy's war effort. Battle honours included the Norwegian campaign in the spring of 1940 and the Battle of Taranto in November 1940, when in one attack 20 Swordfish from HMS *Illustrious* effectively prevented the Italian fleet from participating any further in the war. Other operations included attacks on the *Bismarck,* and on the *Scharnhorst, Gneisenau* and *Prinz Eugen,* after which tragically unsuccessful exploit Lt Cdr Eugene Esmonde was awarded a posthumous VC.

Swordfish continued to operate more or less unchanged right up to the end of the war, a record few of its contemporaries could match. But with the ending of hostilities the Navy lost little time in disposing of this anachronistic old warhorse.

K4305, seen here on floats, was one of two prototype Seafoxes

K4304, seen here at Hamble, was the first prototype Seafox

Fairey Seafox

The Seafox was a two-seat spotter-reconnaissance seaplane designed to be catapulted from light cruisers. Built to Specification 11/32, the prototype flew for the first time on May 27, 1936. It was a conventional two-bay biplane with a fabric-covered all-metal structure.

Although designed to be powered by the 500 hp Bristol Aquila sleeve-valve engine, production aircraft were in fact fitted with the 395 hp Napier Rapier VI, resulting in much reduced performance. A total of 64 production Seafoxes were built between 1936 and 1938, and all but one were completed as seaplanes.

After the usual trials by the MAEE at Felixstowe and catapult trials by the RAE, production Seafoxes were delivered to five reconnaissance catapult flights—Nos 702, 713, 714, 716 and 718—which were later combined to form No 700 Squadron.

Probably the best known operation by the type during the Second World War was the shadowing of the German pocket battleship *Admiral Graf Spee* during mid-December 1939, which resulted in what became known as the Battle of the River Plate.

The last Seafox unit was disbanded in July 1943.

Blackburn Skua

The two-seat Blackburn Skua is notable as the Fleet Air Arm's first operational deck-capable monoplane, although it first flew as late as February 1937. It was also the first British aircraft specifically designed for dive bombing to enter squadron service.

Designed by G. E. Petty to Air Ministry Specification 0.27/34, the B-24 Skua was powered by the 890 hp Bristol Perseus sleeve-valve engine. A production contract to Specification 25/36 for 190 aircraft was placed in July 1936, more than six months before the first flight of the prototype, and first squadron deliveries, to Nos 800 and 803 Squadrons at Worthy Down, were made late in 1938, the Skuas replacing Hawker Nimrods and Ospreys.

With the outbreak of the Second World War the Skuas were soon in action, first blood going to an aircraft of 803 Squadron which shot down a Dornier Do18 flying boat off Norway on September 25, 1939. More dramatic was the sinking in a dive-bombing attack of the German cruiser *Königsberg* in Bergen harbour on April 10, 1940, by 16 aircraft from 800 and 803 Squadrons. Sadly, almost all of these aircraft were lost a few days later during the Narvik operation.

By August 1941 the Skua had been largely replaced in front-line service by the Fairey Fulmar and Hawker Sea Hurricane, though surviving aircraft continued for some years as target tugs.

K5178 was the prototype Skua

With wings folded the Skua was an economical user of limited carrier hangar space

Prototype Skua K5178 during trials

Sea Gladiator N5525 with A-frame hook and dinghy pack under the lower wing centre section

Gloster Sea Gladiator

The Sea Gladiator was a single-seat carrierborne fleet fighter ordered in something of a hurry in 1938 to replace the ageing Hawker Nimrod. The first order, in March 1938, was for 38 aircraft; these were converted from RAF aircraft and designated Sea Gladiator (Interim). Fitted with catapult points, arrester gear and underfuselage collapsible dinghy, they were delivered during December that year, the first 13 aircraft going to Worthy Down for training while the remainder were delivered to 801 Squadron at Donibristle and 804 Squadron at Hatston, and to Eastleigh.

The main production batch of 60 Sea Gladiators, which differed from the Interim aircraft only in minor respects, was ordered in June 1938. Following sea trials on board *Courageous* in March 1939 the first squadrons were embarked for front-line service, initially in *Courageous* and later in *Glorious, Furious* and *Eagle*.

The type saw action in Norway, the Mediterranean and the North Sea, but biplane fighters were no match for the Luftwaffe's monoplanes and the Sea Gladiator had largely been replaced by the Grumman Martlet by the end of 1940.

de Havilland Dominie I NR782, identified as a Culdrose aircraft by the "CU" on its fin

de Havilland Dominie

The Dominie, a military version of the DH.89 Dragon Rapide light commercial biplane, served with both the Royal Air Force and the Royal Navy during and after the Second World War.

The Fleet Air Arm acquired a total of 65 between April 1940 and December 1946, using them for navigation training and communications duties.

Unarmed, they were powered by a pair of 200 hp de Havilland Gipsy Six engines and could carry up to ten people when configured for the communications role.

The last Royal Navy Dominies were disposed of in 1958.

Flight of the Grumman Martlet Is

Grumman Martlet/Wildcat

With the arrival of the Martlet in the early stages of the war the Fleet Air Arm finally had the monoplane fleet fighter that it needed so badly. The Navy had been forced for too long to make do with obsolete biplane types like the Sea Gladiator, with a maximum speed of less than 250 mph, and the four-gun, 300 mph American fighter gladdened the hearts of all but the most entrenched of traditionalists.

The Martlet was the British version of the US Navy's F4F-3, which had first flown in prototype form in September 1937, followed by the first production aircraft in February 1940. The US Navy placed an initial order for 78 to replace its Grumman F3F-3 biplane. At about the same time France ordered 100 under the Grumman company designation G-36A. In June 1940 the collapse of France led to the

entire contract (now reduced to 91 aircraft) being transferred to Britain. The first six aircraft, now named Martlet Is, arrived at Prestwick, Scotland, by sea in August.

The first FAA unit to be equipped was 804 Squadron, which exchanged its Sea Gladiators for Martlets at Hatston in September 1940. This initial batch of Martlets all had non-folding wings and were not suitable for carrier use. The Wildcat II, however, had fully folding wings and was in all respects fully navalised. Like all subsequent versions of the type, the Wildcat II was powered by the 1,200 hp Pratt & Whitney Twin Wasp.

Ordered by Britain during 1940, the first Martlet IIs began to equip FAA squadrons from March the following year. In September 1941 these aircraft became the first of the Martlet

types to be embarked in British aircraft carriers.

No fewer than 13 front-line squadrons used the type, flying off both fleet carriers, such as *Illustrious* and *Victorious,* and the hastily converted ex-merchantman escort carriers, such as *Battler* and *Archer.* Sturdy and manoeuvrable, the Martlet was well liked by its pilots and succeeded in destroying a creditable number of enemy aircraft.

Three further versions served with the Fleet Air Arm during the Second World War: the Martlet IV and V and the Wildcat VI. Unlike earlier versions, which were bought direct by the British Government, the latter marks were supplied by the United States under Lend-Lease arrangements. Although the Martlet IV and V were not renamed Wildcat IV and V until January 1944, they will hereafter be referred to by the later name

Grumman Martlet I AL257

to minimise confusion.

The Wildcat IV was the equivalent of the US Navy's F4F-4 and differed principally in having a total of six wing-mounted 0.50-cal machine guns to the earlier aircraft's four. Deliveries, which amounted to 220, began in 1942.

With the US aircraft industry rapidly gaining momentum the practice of subcontracting became prevalent, as it had been in Britain during the First World War. Thus the Wildcat V, which began to appear in 1943, was built not by Grumman but by General Motors Corporation. The Fleet Air Arm received 312 of the type (known in the US as the FM-1) before the General Motors production line switched to the Wildcat VI (FM-2).

Royal Navy Wildcat IVs and Vs served widely on the MAC ships (Merchant Aircraft Carriers), which were either converted grain carriers or tankers. Nineteen were produced and the smallest boasted a flight deck less than 400ft in length by 62ft wide. Used for convoy escort, the MAC ships usually carried a mix of Swordfish for attacking submarines and Wildcats for fighter protection.

By the middle of 1944 no fewer than 15 FAA squadrons of Wildcat IVs and Vs were engaged in escort work. Later in the summer of 1944 the first of the Wildcat VIs began to appear. These aircraft featured a taller fin and rudder and were powered by the 1,350 hp Wright Cyclone engine. A total of 340 were supplied under Lend-Lease and the majority served in the Far East.

Blackburn Roc L3084 was used by the manufacturer as an engine testbed

Blackburn Roc

The two-seat Roc was designed to meet the requirements of Specification O.30/35, which called for a turret-armed fleet fighter. It was developed from and was structurally similar to the Blackburn Skua and had the same Bristol Perseus engine. Main differences between the two aircraft were the four-gun Boulton-Paul turret, mounted aft of the pilot's cockpit, and the slightly different wing rigging.

A production contract for 136 Rocs, to be built in Boulton-Paul's Wolverhampton factory, was placed in April 1937. The first production aircraft flew on December 23, 1938. After the usual trials, first at Martlesham and later at Boscombe Down (new home of the A & AEE from September 1939), the type was cleared for squadron use, the first-aircraft being allocated to 806 Squadron at Eastleigh in February 1940.

Although designed as a carrierborne aircraft, the Roc never actually operated as such and its entire service career was confined to shore-based operations. Its front-line life was exceptionally short, for the type had been replaced in 806 Squadron by Fulmar Is by July 1940 and in 801 Squadron, which had received its Rocs during June 1940, by Sea Hurricanes only two or three months later. Thereafter the Roc was used entirely by second-line units on anti-aircraft co-operation, target-towing and miscellaneous training duties until the last was retired in August 1943.

Roc with power-operated turret clearly visible

Albacore I N4309 with side access door open

Fairey Albacore

The Albacore single-engined biplane was designed to succeed the Swordfish in the carrierborne torpedo-bomber role. But although it was sound enough in design it did not offer enough in the way of improved performance over the well established Stringbag and was destined to be outlived by the aircraft it should have replaced.

Designed to Specification S.41/36, issued in February 1937, it incorporated a number of apparently desirable features such as enclosed and heated cockpits, automatic dinghy-launching system and hydraulic wing flaps. It was powered by the 1,065 hp Bristol Taurus II, later to be replaced by the 1,130 hp Taurus XII. Principal

weapon was the 1,600lb Mk XIIA 18in torpedo.

The prototype, L7074, flew for the first time on December 12, 1938. A contract for 100 aircraft (to include two prototypes) had been placed in May 1937 and these were all built at Fairey's factory at Hayes, Middlesex. Ultimately a total of 800 were built, production ending in 1943.

The Albacore entered service with 826 Squadron, which commissioned at Ford, Sussex, in March 1940. Throughout the remainder of the year Albacores continued to operate as land-based aircraft, carrying out bombing and minelaying raids, sometimes under the control of RAF Coastal Command.

The first squadrons to embark on a carrier were Nos 826 and 829 Squadrons, which joined HMS *Formidable* in November 1940. At the peak of its career, in 1942, some 15 FAA squadrons were equipped with the Albacore, plus one RAF and one RCAF squadron.

By late 1943, however, most of the FAA units had been re-equipped with the Barracuda or, as in the case of 832 Squadron, the Grumman Avenger. In fact the last unit to fly the Albacore operationally was to be the RCAF squadron, which was engaged in anti-shipping operations from Manston until shortly after the D-Day landings in Normandy.

Well worn Albacore I, probably L7075, on test flight

Albacores of 820 Squadron on board HMS *Victorious*

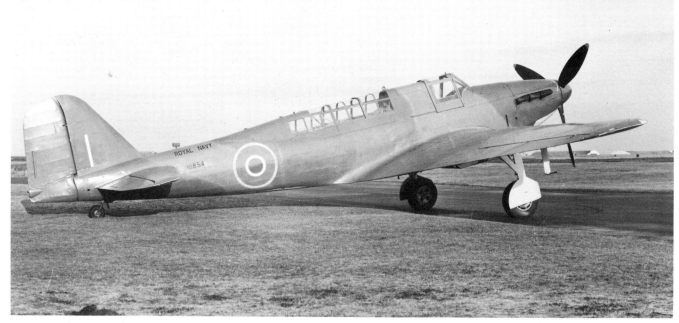

Fulmar N1854 was the first production aircraft. It was retained by Fairey and registered G-AIBE after the war

Fairey Fulmar

The Fulmar was a single-engined two-seat fleet fighter designed to Specification O.8/38. Essentially a development of Fairey's day bomber for the RAF, built to Specification P.4/34, the Fulmar was conceived as a two-seater primarily because the shipborne navigational aids of the day were so rudimentary that naval pilots had to be assisted by a navigator if they were to have any chance of finding the carrier in poor weather or at night.

The prototype P.4/34, K5099, flew for the first time on January 13, 1937, powered by a 1,030 hp Rolls-Royce Merlin II. Following instructions to proceed on the naval fighter development issued in May 1938, the first true prototype Fulmar, N1854, flew for the first time on January 4, 1940, powered by a 1,080 hp Merlin VIII.

Production of Fulmar Is totalled 250 aircraft, all built at Stockport. Substitution of the 1,300 hp Merlin XXX for the VIII characterised the Fulmar II, the first of which flew in January 1941. A total of 350 were completed, the last being delivered in February 1943.

The first Fulmar Is equipped 808 Squadron at Worthy Down in June 1940, this unit later embarking in HMS *Ark Royal* for escort duties with Malta convoys. By September that year two further squadrons had been equipped, 806 Squadron replacing its Skuas and Rocs at Eastleigh in July and 807 forming at Worthy Down in September.

The peak of the Fulmar's career came during 1942, when some 14 squadrons operated the type, but by the beginning of 1943 it was rapidly being superseded by the Seafire. A handful of night-fighter Fulmars continued to operate until as late as March 1945.

Fulmar II

Curtiss Seamew FN475

Curtiss Seamew

First flown in the United States as the XSO3C-1 in October 1939, the Curtiss Seamew was acquired by the Fleet Air Arm as a catapult-launched two-seat reconnaissance aircraft.

Powered by a 520 hp Ranger engine, the Seamew offered only modest performance and was destined to see no operational service with the Royal Navy. A total of about 800 Seamews were built during 1941 and 1942, and some 250 were to have been delivered to the Fleet Air Arm under Lend-Lease. But it is believed that only about 100 reached Britain, where they were designated Seamew I.

Royal Navy aircraft served almost exclusively in the training role, both in Britain and in Canada. In addition to the standard aircraft, which could be fitted with either a narrow-track fixed undercarriage or floats, the Royal Navy also took delivery of a small number of radio-controlled target-drone aircraft designated Queen Seamew.

Hawker Sea Hurricane IIC photographed in April 1943

Hawker Sea Hurricane

Like its contemporary the
Spitfire, the Hawker Hurricane
was destined to make a
relatively simple transition from
land-based to shipborne fighter.
The feasibility of operating the
type from a carrier deck was first
proved during May 1940 when
Hurricanes were operated from
HMS *Glorious* during the
ill-fated Norwegian campaign.
The success of this
operation—so far as the
Hurricane was
concerned—resulted in the
production of the first Sea
Hurricane Mk IA. The prototype,
a modified Hurricane I, was
equipped with both catapult
spools and an arrester hook,
though the first 50 production
aircraft were delivered hookless.

These Sea Hurricane IAs were

earmarked for operation as
"Catafighters," an extremely
hazardous operation which
involved their being catapulted
from the foredecks of Catapult
Aircraft Merchantmen, created
specifically to counter the threat
posed to convoys by the
Luftwaffe's long-range
Focke-Wulf Condors. Once in
the air the Hurricanes generally
had no carrier to land back on,
and the pilots were faced with
the choice of either baling out or
ditching their aircraft as close as
possible to a friendly ship.

The Sea Hurricane IBs,
converted like the IAs from
former land-based Hurricane Is,
were fully navalised and carried
the standard eight-gun
armament. In addition to the Mk
IBs, some 25 Hurricane IIA

Series 2s were similarly
converted.

The Sea Hurricane IB was first
embarked during October 1941
aboard the first of the
MAC-ships, converted from
merchantmen and provided
with a small flight deck but no
hangar. Prime task of these
vessels and their tiny
complement of fighters and
anti-submarine aircraft was
convoy escort.

Later Sea Hurricane variants
were the Mk IC, armed with four
20mm wing-mounted cannon,
and the Mk IIC with the Merlin
XX engine. Final variant was the
Sea Hurricane XIIA, converted
from Canadian-built aircraft and
powered by the Packard-built
Merlin XXIX.

It is not known just how many

Sea Hurricanes were delivered
to the Fleet Air Arm during the
Second World War, but records
reveal that contracts for some
800 conversions were issued.
The final aircraft was delivered
in August 1943. By the end of
that year, however, the type was
rapidly being superseded in
front-line service by Seafires
and Hellcats aboard the larger
carriers and by Wildcats in the
escort carriers.

Some 19 Fleet Air Arm
squadrons were equipped with
the Sea Hurricane at some time
or another, and it is generally
accepted that this hardy fighter
played a major role in protecting
the vital convoy routes,
particularly between Britain and
Russia, at a crucial point in the
war.

Seafire L.IIC lands aboard HMS *Furious*

Seafire III showing extent of wing-folding for stowage

Supermarine Seafire (Merlin)

Before Supermarine began building the true Seafire carrierborne fighter, the Royal Navy had carried out a number of trials aboard HMS *Illustrious* during 1941 using RAF Spitfire VBs fitted with arrester hooks. The success of these experiments led to the conversion of 48 Spitfire VBs into Seafire IBs. Almost the only modification made was the provision of a V-frame arrester hook. The majority of the conversions were carried out by Air Services Training at Hamble, and a further 118 aircraft were later converted. All had non-folding "B" wings fitted with two cannon and four machine guns.

The Seafire IIC, deliveries of which began in September 1942, used the "C" wing with the "Universal" armament option of four cannon or any of the earlier cannon/machine gun combinations. The IIC also incorporated local airframe strengthening to permit installation of catapult spools and rocket-assisted take-off gear (RATOG). Three versions were produced: the L.IIC for low-altitude operations and fitted with the Merlin 32 engine driving a four-bladed propeller, the standard F.IIC and the photo-reconnaissance PR.IIC.

Total production amounted to some 400 aircraft, 260 of which were built by Supermarine and the remaining 140 by Westland.

Major production version of the Merlin-engined Seafires was the Seafire III, which, like the Mk II, was produced in three sub-variants. All Mk IIIs incorporated for the first time the facility of wing-folding. Production by Cunliffe-Owen Aircraft and Westland Aircraft Ltd began in April 1943, and between them the two companies turned out more than 1,100.

First introduced into Fleet Air Arm service in June 1942, the Merlin-engined Seafire was operational in almost all of the major theatres of war, beginning with Operation Torch, the Allied invasion of North Africa, and continuing through to the final operations against the Japanese in the Pacific in the summer of 1945.

By the end of the Second World War the Seafire II and III were being superseded by the Griffon-engined Seafire XV, though at the time of VJ-Day eight out of 12 front-line Seafire squadrons were still equipped with the earlier aircraft. The last Seafire III was retired by 759 Squadron at Yeovilton in 1946.

Westland-built Seafire L.III PP979 comes to grief in a landing accident aboard an escort carrier

Vought-Sikorsky Chesapeake I at Lee-on-Solent

Vought-Sikorsky Chesapeake

The two-seat Chesapeake was the Fleet Air Arm's version of the Vought SB2U Vindicator. First flown on January 4, 1936, the SB2U-1 entered squadron service with the US Navy in December 1937.

First export sales were to France, which had received a number of the type when invaded by Germany in 1940. Britain elected to take over the balance of the French order, which amounted to some 50 aircraft. Designated Chesapeake I, they incorporated minor modifications to suit them for operations from British aircraft carriers. The first examples arrived early in 1941 and first equipped No 728 Squadron at Arbroath. The first operational squadron was No 811 at Lee-on-Solent, which took delivery in July that year.

Because of its long take-off run the Chesapeake was not suitable for operation from the escort carriers for which the Royal Navy had intended it, and it was soon relegated to training duties.

Powerplant was a 750 hp Pratt & Whitney Twin Wasp Junior, and when configured as a dive bomber the Chesapeake could carry a total of 1,500lb of bombs.

Vought-Sikorsky Kingfisher

Vought-Sikorsky Kingfisher

The two-seat Kingfisher reconnaissance aircraft was developed in the United States by Vought-Sikorsky under a contract awarded by the US Navy in March 1937. Designated XOS2U-1, the prototype flew for the first time on July 20, 1938, powered by a 450 hp Pratt & Whitney R-985-4 engine. The first production examples were delivered to the US Navy in August 1940.

The Fleet Air Arm received its Kingfishers under Lend-Lease arrangements, starting in the summer of 1942. Total deliveries reached 100 aircraft, configured either as conventional landplanes with tricycle undercarriage or as seaplanes with one large float under the belly and two smaller stabilising floats, one under each wingtip. Armament consisted of a single fixed 0.30-cal machine gun firing forward and one free-mounted gun aft. Up to 240lb of bombs could be carried beneath the wings.

In Royal Navy service Kingfishers were deployed on armed merchant cruisers such as HMS *Cilicia, Corfu* and *Canton,* and on cruisers such as *Emerald* and *Enterprise.*

Barracuda II P9687

Fairey Barracuda

The Royal Navy operated four versions of Fairey's angular Barracuda and the type remained in service in one form or another (albeit with a short post-war break) from January 1943 until 1953. Even if it was not the best-looking aircraft ever to be foisted upon a long-suffering Fleet Air Arm, it won respect for its prodigious load-carrying capability, if not for its handling qualities.

Designed to meet the requirements of Specification S.24/37, the Fairey Type 100, as the Barracuda was originally known, was intended as a replacement for the Albacore biplane torpedo bomber.

The prototype, P1767, flew for the first time on December 7, 1940. But because of the pressure of more urgent calls for

other types of combat aircraft the design effectively remained on the shelf for a further two years, although a second prototype, P1770, flew in June 1941.

Series production of the Barracuda I began in early 1942 and the first production aircraft flew on May 18 that year. Only 25, powered by the 1,260 hp Rolls-Royce Merlin 30, were built.

The Barracuda II was powered by the 1,640 hp Merlin 32. Production began during the latter part of 1942 at Fairey's Stockport factory, Blackburn at Brough, and Boulton and Paul at Wolverhampton.

Last of the wartime Barracudas was the Mk III, generally similar to the Mk II but equipped with ASV Mk X radar

for anti-submarine reconnaissance.

Total production of the Mks I, II and III was 2,572 aircraft, the majority of which were Mk IIs. The first of this variant entered service with 827 Squadron in January 1943 and a year later the Barracuda establishment in the Royal Navy had grown to 12 front-line squadrons.

Although originally conceived as a torpedo bomber, the aircraft will be best remembered as a dive bomber. One of the most famous Barracuda actions was the series of dive-bombing attacks against the German battleship *Tirpitz* in Kaafiord, Norway, between April and August 1944.

After VJ-Day most Barracuda squadrons were disbanded,

with only three remaining operational by the beginning of 1946.

A small force of Barracuda IIIs was formed in 1947 to perform the anti-submarine patrol role until the arrival of the Grumman Avenger in 1953.

Last of all the Barracuda variants was the Mk V, which entered service in 1947. It was an almost entirely new aircraft, powered by a 2,020 hp Rolls-Royce Griffon in place of the earlier versions' Merlin and featuring wings and vertical tail of substantially altered shape.

Only about 30 were built and none was to enter front-line service, the aircraft equipping only 750 Squadron at St Merryn and 783 Squadron at RNAS Lee-on-Solent.

DP855, photographed in February 1944, was a TR.III

Ultimate Barracuda, the Mk V. RK558 is from RNAS Lee-on-Solent

The Avenger I was orignally designated Tarpon in Fleet Air Arm service

Avenger III KE461

Grumman Avenger

The Avenger was used by the Fleet Air Arm in four versions: the TR.I, TR.II, TR.III and AS.4. Built by Grumman in the USA, the Avenger first flew in 1941 under the designation XTBF-1 and was intended to be a replacement for the Douglas Devastator torpedo bomber in US Navy service.

The first production TBF-1s entered US Navy squadrons in the spring of 1942, but the Fleet Air Arm did not receive its first Lend-Lease aircraft until the following year, initially under the name Tarpon (changed back to the original American name in January 1944). A total of 402 Avenger Is, the equivalent of US Navy TBF-1s, were delivered. These were followed by 334 General Motors-built Avenger IIs, equivalent to the TBM-1. Last of the torpedo-bomber variants supplied were the 222 Avenger IIIs (TBM-3). A batch of 70 Avenger IVs was allocated to the Fleet Air Arm but not delivered.

The first Royal Navy squadron to be equipped was 832 Squadron, which embarked on USS *Saratoga* in April 1943 and shortly afterwards helped support the landings in the Solomon Isles. The squadron later transferred to the British carrier HMS *Victorious*.

Most FAA Avengers were used as bombers, carrying up to 2,000lb of internal ordnance, or as strike aircraft carrying up to eight 60lb rockets beneath the wings. They were widely deployed throughout several theatres of war, engaging in anti-shipping strikes before the Normandy landings in June 1944 and carrying out arduous bombing attacks against Japanese targets in the Far East campaign. In fact, more Fleet Air Arm Avengers served in the Pacific than elsewhere. With the end of the war Avengers were rapidly withdrawn from front-line use, with only two squadrons operational by the

end of 1945.

The last of this series of Avengers left FAA service with the disbandment of 828 Squadron in June 1946. The type did not wear Royal Navy colours again until 1953, when the altogether different Avenger AS.4 entered service.

The AS.4 was based on the Avenger III airframe. The type was ordered as an interim anti-submarine strike aircraft pending the availability of the first Fairey Gannet AS.1s. A total of 100 were supplied by the US under the Mutual Defence Assistance Programme and the first arrived in Britain aboard the carrier *Perseus* in March 1953, entering service with 813 Squadron in May that year.

The AS.4 superseded the Barracuda and Firefly in the carrierborne anti-submarine role in five front-line squadrons until 1955, and afterwards with three RNVR squadrons until their disbandment.

Vought Corsair

One of the outstanding aircraft of the Second World War, the Corsair was at first treated with some suspicion, even outright dislike, by Royal Navy pilots. But it ultimately became one of the Fleet Air Arm's most widely deployed fleet fighters.

The history of the aircraft goes back to January 1938, when the original V-166B fighter proposal was submitted. In June that year the US Navy awarded a contract for a prototype XF4U-1. The main principle of the Vought engineers in formulating the Corsair's design was to take the most powerful engine then available and mate it to the slimmest possible fuselage to produce minimum drag. The need for ground clearance for the vast propeller caused designer Rex Beisel to adopt the unique inverted gull-wing layout.

The XF4U-1 flew for the first time on May 29, 1940, and in October that year exceeded 400 mph in level flight, the first fighter in the world to do so. First production contracts, for 584 aircraft, were awarded in June 1941 and the first front-line US Navy unit to receive its Corsairs was equipped during the following summer.

Lend-Lease deliveries to the Fleet Air Arm began during 1943, with the first squadron, No 1830, forming in the US on June 1 with the Corsair I, equivalent to the US Navy's F4U-4. By the end of the year there were eight FAA Corsair squadrons, each of which formed and worked up in the US before embarking in British escort carriers. A total of 2,012 were allocated to the Fleet Air Arm and the last of 19 squadrons formed in early 1945.

Beginning with the Corsair II, the British clipped 8in off each wing tip to facilitate storage aboard the smaller Royal Navy carriers. Other modifications included a revised cockpit canopy and the provision of underwing hardpoints for carrying up to 2,000lb of bombs or 470gal of fuel in long-range tanks.

As with all Lend-Lease squadrons, the end of the war brought rapid disbandment and only four remained in commission by the end of 1945; all had gone by the following August.

Goodyear-built Corsair IV

Corsair III

Blackburn Firebrand

The single-seat Blackburn Firebrand was a fighter of epic proportions which should have made a great contribution to the Fleet Air Arm's war effort but which, for a variety of reasons, did not become available for squadron use until late in 1945.

The type had its origins in Air Ministry Specification N.8/39, the first of two intended to produce a successor to the Gloster Gladiator, Blackburn Skua and Fairey Fulmar. Specification N.8/39 and the subsequent N.9/39 differed only in details of gun installation, but both called for a two-seat aircraft. N.9/39 eventually became N.5/40 and was admirably met by the Fairey Firefly, while N.8/39 underwent a traumatic metamorphosis to emerge as N.11/40, in which form it called for a single-seat aircraft. Both Hawker and Blackburn fielded competitors: Hawker's was the P.1009, a folding-wing version of the Typhoon, while the winner from Blackburn was the Napier Sabre-powered B-37, which flew for the first time on February 27, 1942.

Following contractor's trials at Brough a number of aerodynamic modifications were made, delaying the first deck-landing trials until February 1943. Then began a bewildering series of engine and airframe changes and modifications which effectively scotched the Firebrand's chances of seeing squadron service during the war, at least in its intended role of fleet fighter. However, the type's potential as a high-speed torpedo-carrying strike aircraft had not been overlooked and, after nine of the F.1 version had been completed, attention was switched to the TF.2. Blackburn completed only 12, the first of which emerged in March 1943. But none was destined to enter a front-line squadron, the aircraft going instead to 708 Squadron at RNAS Lee-on-Solent, where they were used for a variety of trials.

Installation of the 2,400 hp Bristol Centaurus sleeve-valve engine resulted in a major redesign of the airframe, culminating in the redesignation of the aircraft as the Blackburn B-45 Firebrand TF.III. First flight of this variant was in December 1943 but the first of only 27 production aircraft did not fly until the following November, by which time the war in Europe had but a few months to run. In any case, none of these aircraft was to see operational use as most were, again, used for various tests and experiments.

Next variant to emerge was the B-46 Firebrand TF.IV (redesignated Mk 4 in 1948 in the reorganisation of British service aircraft numbering). No fewer than 102 were to be built, and the first flew for the first time in May 1945. The Firebrand finally reached an operational unit when 813 Squadron was reformed with the type at RNAS Ford on September 1, 1945.

The last two production variants were the Mks 5 and 5A, some 68 of which were built. These incorporated a number of control improvements which rendered the aircraft both safe and pleasant to fly, despite its great bulk. Although the Firebrand was embarked in both HMS *Illustrious* and *Eagle* it was not used during the Korean War. The last Firebrands were retired during 1953 following the introduction of the Fleet Air Arm's last propeller-driven strike fighter, the equally formidable Westland Wyvern.

The definitive Firebrand, the TF.5

A TF.5 loses its hook and
engages the barrier

Grumman Hellcat

Although bearing a more than superficial resemblance to the F4F Wildcat which it was intended to replace, the F6F Hellcat was an altogether larger aircraft powered by a 2,000 hp Pratt & Whitney R-2800 Double Wasp engine. Performance was also substantially improved, although firepower remained unchanged.

The first Hellcats entered service with the US Navy at the end of 1942 and by the middle of the following year they were widely deployed throughout the Pacific fleet.

Hellcats were supplied to Britain under Lend-Lease from the spring of 1943, and when deliveries finished at the end of the war a total of 1,182 had been allocated. This total broke down as 252 Hellcat Is, equivalent to the US Navy's F6F-3, and 930 Hellcat IIs, the equivalent of the F6F-5. More than 70 Hellcat IIs were configured as night

fighters and carried the APS-6 radar in a pod mounted on the starboard wing. These aircraft were the equivalent of the US Navy's F6F-5N.

Hellcats first entered service with the Royal Navy when 800 Squadron gave up its Sea Hurricanes in July 1943. First shipboard duty was aboard the escort carrier HMS *Emperor*, carrying out anti-shipping strikes off the coast of Norway. Like those of the US Navy, however, most FAA Hellcats served in the Pacific.

In the later stages of the Pacific war FAA Hellcats began increasingly to replace Wildcats embarked in the light escort carriers. By VJ-Day there were 12 squadrons of Hellcats, including the two night-fighter units, Nos 891 and 892 Squadrons. At the end of the war most surviving aircraft were returned to the US under the terms of Lend-Lease.

Hellcat FR.2 JV270

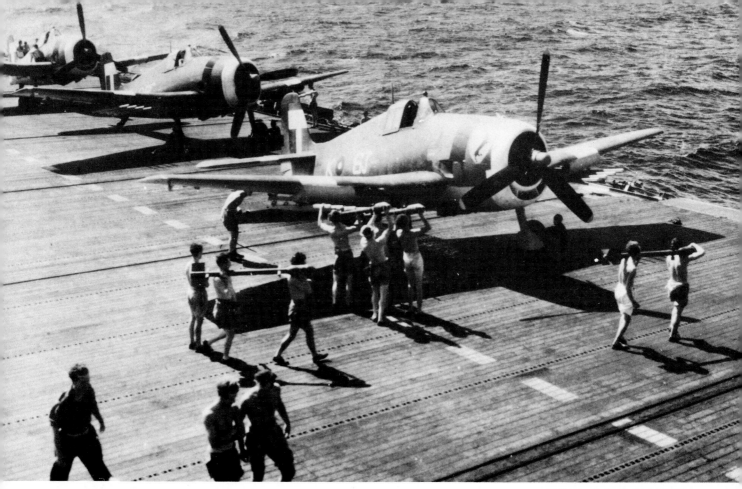

Hellcats of the British Pacific
Fleet on board an escort carrier

Fairey Firefly

Although there was some outward similarity between the two-seat Griffon-engined Firefly and the Merlin-engined Fulmar which preceded it, the Firefly, designed to Naval Specification N.5/40, sprang from a different line. Designed initially to combine the roles of fighter and reconnaissance aircraft, the Firefly was significantly faster than the Fulmar and, armed with four wing-mounted 20mm cannon, somewhat harder-hitting.

A bewildering variety of variants were produced over a period spanning more than 10 years. The first of these was the F.1 day fighter, followed by the radar-equipped FR.1 and the NF.1, a night-fighter variant of the FR.1. In between came the F.1A, which was an F.1 brought up to FR.1 standard. Also broadly similar were the dual-control T.1 and the TT.1 target-towing gunnery trainer.

The Firefly 2 series consisted of the NF.2 (confusingly, this radar-equipped night fighter was produced before the NF.1) and the dual-controlled T.2. The Firefly Mk 3 was a Mk 1 fitted with the Rolls-Royce Griffon 61,

and was distinguished by its characteristic chin radiator.

The Mk 4 appeared towards the end of the Second World War and introduced the first major aerodynamic change, a new clipped wing with forward extensions to the inboard leading edge to house the radiators for the 2,250 hp Griffon 74 engine. Tail area was increased slightly and two underwing pods were carried, one containing fuel and the other the radar scanner. Three Mk 4 variants were produced: the FR. 4, the NF.4 night fighter and the target-tug TT.4.

The Firefly 5s and the Mk 6 were aerodynamically similar to the Mk 4 series but introduced changes to the operational equipment. The series consisted of the FR.5, designed for day fighter-reconnaissance, the night-fighter NF.5, the anti-submarine AS.5 equipped with sonobuoys, and the T.5, an Australian conversion of the FR.5 for the Royal Australian Navy. The only Mk 6 variant was the unarmed AS.6 anti-submarine aircraft.

The Mk 7s, which first appeared in 1951, are detailed separately in this book.

The prototype Firefly, Z1826, flew for the first time on December 22, 1941, and was the forerunner of an initial production batch of 200 F.1s. When production ended in 1946 more than 870 Mk 1s and their derivatives had been built. Production of the Mk 4 series was relatively limited, amounting to only 160 aircraft, but the externally similar Mks 5 and 6 reached a total of 485 aircraft by the time production ended in 1951.

The exploits of the Firefly series are too numerous and widespread to be summarised here, other than to note that the principal areas of operation of early-series aircraft during the Second World War were the Far East and Pacific, while later marks were employed extensively during the Korean War in the early 1950s.

A total of 22 front-line Fleet Air Arm squadrons were equipped with the type, as well as seven training and one communications squadron. The last variant in Royal Navy service was the AS.6, the last of which was withdrawn in 1956 following the introduction of the first Gannets and Avengers.

Firefly I under control of DLCO, the deck landing control officer or "bats"

Firefly AS.6 VT406

Unscheduled arrival by a Firefly AS.6, which has taken the barrier. Pieces of radome from the pod under the starboard wing litter the deck

Supermarine Seafire (Griffon)

The first of the Griffon-engined Seafires was the Mk XV, which entered service with the Fleet Air Arm as the Second World War drew to a close.

Developed to Specification N.4/43, the three prototypes flew for the first time during 1944. A total of 384 were built, 134 by Cunliffe-Owen Aircraft Ltd and 250 by Westland. Apart from the engine cowling contours there was not a great deal of external difference between the Mk XV and the Merlin-engined Mk III. The new aircraft did have increased internal fuel capacity, however, and from the 51st aircraft the V-frame arrester hook was replaced by a "sting"-type hook mounted in the extreme tail.

The type first entered service with 802 Squadron at Arbroath in May 1945. Three additional Seafire XV squadrons, Nos 803, 805 and 806, were commissioned. In addition to service aboard the wartime escort carriers *Premier, Berwick* and *Vengeance,* the Mk XV also served for a time aboard the post-war light fleet carriers *Ocean* and *Glory.*

Next version to be produced was the Mk XVII. This was a developed version of the XV; the prototype, NS493, which flew for the first time during 1945, had been the third prototype Mk XV.

The Seafire XVII was the first model to feature a bubble canopy with cutaway rear-fuselage top decking. Total production was 232 aircraft in two sub-variants, the F.XVII and the FR.XVII fighter-reconnaissance model.

The Mk XVII proved to be the longest-lived of the Griffon Seafires, the last remaining unit, No 764 Squadron, retiring the last of its aircraft at Yeovilton in November 1954.

The last three versions to be built were the Seafire 45, 46 and 47, based respectively on the RAF's Spitfire 21, 22 and 24.

The Seafire 45, which was produced to Specification N.7/44, retained the old-style hood of the Spitfire 21 and, powered by the Griffon Series 61/85, was fitted with a vast five-bladed propeller. Only 50 were built, all by Vickers-Armstrongs at Castle Bromwich, and the variant never entered service with front-line squadrons, being used only by 778 Squadron at Ford.

The Seafire 46 reintroduced the bubble canopy and cut-down rear fuselage, and later production aircraft had the tall fin and rudder of the Spitfire 24. Production totalled only 24 aircraft, the end of the war resulting in the pruning of an original order for 200. Like the Mk 45, the Seafire 46 did not see front-line service. The only units to be equipped were 781 Squadron at Lee-on-Solent, from March 1947, and No 1832 RNVR Squadron at Culham in July that year.

Whereas the Mk 45 and Mk 46 were not fully deck-capable and remained land-based, the last of the Seafires, the Mk 47, was completely navalised with single-point wing-folding, "sting"-type arrester hook and full operational equipment. The original production contract for the Mk 47 was for 150 aircraft, but with the imminence of the new generation of jet-powered aircraft this was cut back to just 90, the first of which entered service with 804 Squadron at Ford in February 1948.

The Seafire 47 was operational against communist guerillas in Malaya during 1949 and 1950 and, with 800 Squadron embarked in HMS *Triumph,* in the Korean War. The type was progressively withdrawn from front-line squadrons from 1951 following the arrival of the Attacker but continued with RNVR units until the following year.

Seafire XV SR449, first of the Griffon-engined variants

TM379 was the prototype Seafire F.45

LA542 was similar to the ultimate Seafire variant, the Mk 47, except that it featured non-folding wings

Supermarine Sea Otter ASR.II RD872

Vickers-Supermarine Sea Otter

The Sea Otter, the last biplane to be designed by Supermarine, was a carrierborne or shore-based amphibian which carried a crew of three or four and was designed to replace the venerable Walrus in Fleet Air Arm SAR and communications squadrons.

Designed to Specification S.7/38, the Sea Otter was constructed from wood and metal and was powered by a single 855 hp Bristol Mercury XXX radial engine. Like the Walrus, the Sea Otter had a retractable undercarriage, but with the distinct advantage of hydraulic operation.

The prototype, K8854, flew for the first time in August 1938 as the Supermarine Type 309 and was successively modified to the requirements of Specifications S.14/39 and S.12/40, emerging finally as the Supermarine Type 347.

Production began at Saunders-Roe during 1943, with the first aircraft being completed in July that year. But the type did not enter service with the Fleet Air Arm until November 1944, when six were delivered to No 1700 Squadron at Lee-on-Solent for use aboard the escort carrier HMS *Khedive*. In addition to 1700 Squadron, Nos 1701, 1702 and 1703 Squadrons used the Sea Otter, as did No 772 Fleet Requirements Unit.

de Havilland Sea Mosquito

The de Havilland Mosquito is generally regarded as an exclusively RAF-operated aircraft. But lesser known, if no less useful, variants also served with the Fleet Air Arm during and immediately after the Second World War.

The Sea Mosquito was the result of Admiralty Specification N.15/44, the first to be issued for a twin-engined carrierborne aircraft, and the prototype was a navalised Mosquito FB.IV. It was with this aircraft that Lt Cdr E. M.

"Winkle" Brown made the first deck landing with a British twin-engined aircraft, on HMS *Indefatigable* on March 25, 1944.

Production aircraft, which featured folding wings in addition to deck arrester gear, were designated Sea Mosquito TR.33, and the first of these flew on November 10, 1945. First unit to be equipped was 811 Squadron at Ford, in August 1946. Service life was short, however, for 811 (by then based at RNAS Brawdy in South

Wales) was disbanded in July 1947.

In all, some 50 TR.33s were built out of original Admiralty contracts for 97. The Royal Navy also received six examples of the Sea Mosquito TR.37 fitted with nose-mounted ASV radar, and these were used by 703 Squadron.

In addition to its TR Sea Mosquitoes the Fleet Air Arm also operated small quantities of other versions of the Mosquito, including the Mk VI, which had

Torpedo-armed Sea Mosquito TR.33

Miles Monitor

The twin-engined, two-seat Monitor was designed to meet the requirements of Air Ministry Specification Q.9/42 for a high-speed target tug for the RAF. While design work was under way, however, it was decided that the needs of the Royal Navy were more pressing and the contract was revised to incorporate a number of naval accoutrements.

Powered by a pair of 1,750 hp Wright Double Cyclone engines, the prototype flew for the first time at Woodley on April 5, 1944.

The original production contract was for 600 aircraft, but with the end of the war obviously close at hand the order was cut to 200. Later still it was pruned to only 50, and when 20 had been completed the programme was cancelled altogether. Only ten aircraft were eventually delivered to the Royal Navy and these, designated Monitor TT.II, served briefly with fleet requirements units before being superseded by the Mosquito TT.39. The remaining ten Monitors were meanwhile broken up.

Miles Monitor TT.II

preceded 811 Squadron's TR.33s at Ford between September 1945 and the following August. Intended for familiarisation flying, the Mk IVs remained shore-based and were not equipped for carrier operation.

Other naval Mosquitoes were the T.3 dual-control trainer, acquired in small numbers from the RAF, and the TT.39, a high-speed shore-based target tug that replaced the Miles Monitors in fleet requirements units from about 1948.

Shore-based Mosquito TT.39 target tug

Sikorsky Hoverfly

Up until quite late in the war the Royal Navy had shown little interest in the pioneering work on helicopters being undertaken in the USA. It was not until the emergence of the Sikorsky YR-4A that the potential of these curious flying machines dawned on the Admiralty.

After a short evaluation period the Navy ordered 250 under the designation Hoverfly I. In the event, only 52 were delivered, under Lend-Lease arrangements, and the first of these entered service with No 771 Fleet Requirements Unit at Portland in September 1945 and with 705 Squadron at Gosport. Powered by the 180 hp Warner engine, they had only modest performance, particularly in the hover. But the groundwork for a highly efficient naval helicopter force was laid by these early aircraft and the Hoverfly rightly deserves recognition in Fleet Air Arm history.

The Fleet Air Arm also received 15 Hoverfly IIs. Also supplied under Lend-Lease, in 1946, they served briefly on training and communications duties before being superseded by the much more advanced Dragonfly and Whirlwind.

Ultimate Spitfire development, the Griffon 87-powered Seafang 32 never entered front-line service

Supermarine Seafang

To most eyes the Seafang was the zenith of piston-engined fighter design. It was large, sleek, heavily armed and possessed of a formidable performance. Yet it never entered squadron service with the Fleet Air Arm for, as with so many aircraft whose design and early development coincided with the end of the Second World War, it had been overtaken by technical events—notably the emergence of a practical gas-turbine engine—and was condemned to almost instant obsolescence.

In 1943 Supermarine proposed a laminar-wing Seafire to be powered by the powerful Rolls-Royce Griffon. Designated Supermarine Type 382, it failed to gain the attention of the Air Ministry until 1945, when Specification N.5/45 was issued and, on April 21 of that year, two Seafang prototypes were ordered. In May the Ministry of Aircraft Production (MAP) ordered 150 production aircraft. The first production Seafang, the F.31 (Seafang variants were numbered in the Spitfire/Seafire series) had no wing-fold mechanism, while the fully navalised version, the F.32, had a new system in which only the tips folded.

Deck-landing trials were carried out on HMS *Illustrious* in May 1947. However, the original production order was cut and only nine aircraft, none of which saw operational service, were eventually completed.

Sea Hornet F.20s from the naval air station at Hal Far, Malta

de Havilland Sea Hornet

The Sea Hornet had its genesis in a private-venture proposal for a long-range fighter-bomber which de Havilland had in mind for operations against the Japanese in the later stages of the Second World War. Built to Specification N.5/44, the first prototype Sea Hornet flew for the first time on April 19, 1945. This aircraft was a converted Hornet I and did not incorporate folding wings.

Following deck-landing trials on HMS *Ocean,* which began in August 1945, production contracts were let for the Sea Hornet F.20. When production ended in June 1951 a total of 78 had been completed.

Service trials were carried out at Lee-on-Solent by 703 Squadron in the latter part of 1946. First front-line unit to be equipped was 801 Squadron, initially at Ford. The squadron eventually embarked in HMS *Implacable* in 1949.

In addition to 801, several other FAA squadrons used limited numbers of F.20s, including 806 Squadron, which formed a composite aerobatic team with two Sea Hornets, two Sea Furies and a Sea Vampire. Also equipped was 809 Squadron, with four F.20s on strength.

After 1951 the type was relegated to second-line status

and examples served with fleet requirements units in Malta and at Hurn until 1955.

The other single-seat variant used by the Royal Navy was the PR.22, some 43 of which were acquired for use by 801 and 738 Squadrons. They were generally similar to the F.20s but carried two F.52 cameras (day reconnaissance) or one Fairchild F.19B camera (night reconnaissance) in place of the gun armament.

The only two-seat version of the Sea Hornet was the NF.21, a carrierborne night fighter/all-weather strike fighter. Produced to Specification N.21/45, it was equipped with an

ASH radar scanner in a thimble nose and a separate observer's cockpit placed over the wing trailing edge.

The prototype flew for the first time on July 9, 1946, and after service trials the type entered front-line service with 809 Squadron, which formed at Culdrose in January 1949.

Sea Hornet NF.21s embarked at various times on the carriers *Vengeance, Indomitable* and *Eagle.* Retired from front-line squadrons in 1954, they were used on radar training duties until most were broken up at Yeovilton in 1956. Total production amounted to 79.

An F.20, with A-frame hook lowered, prepares to land on

Sea Hornet NF.21, showing nose-mounted thimble radome and four underfuselage cannon

Sea Hornet NF.21 discards its undercarriage in a dramatic landing accident

Sea Fury FB.II VX639

Sea Fury prototype SR666 during deck-landing trials

Hawker Sea Fury

The single-seat Sea Fury represented the end of an era for the Royal Navy. The last piston-engined fighter to serve with the Fleet Air Arm, it was also, to most eyes, the most beautiful, and it carried Royal Navy colours in both front-line and reserve squadrons from 1947 to 1957.

The Sea Fury was descended from a long line of classic Sidney Camm-designed fighters, but its immediate progenitor was the wickedly efficient Tempest, which the Royal Air Force had been operating since 1944. Discussions of the possibility of producing a smaller and lighter version of the Tempest led to a design to Specification F.6/42 (Tempest Light Fighter [Centaurus]). This became Specification F.2/43 and in 1943 it was suggested that this design, with suitably uprated engine, would also be capable of

Sea Fury FB.IIs

meeting Naval Specification N.7/43.

By December 1943 six prototypes had been ordered with three different powerplants, two Centaurus variants and one Griffon. Early the following year the naval requirement crystallised as Specification N.22/43, and by April 1944 production contracts for 200 F.2/43s for the RAF and 200 naval N.22/43s had been placed.

First to fly was NX798, the prototype F.2/43, on September 1, 1944, powered by a Bristol Centaurus XII driving a four-bladed propeller. This was followed by a Griffon-powered prototype in November.

The first prototype Sea Fury (as the naval aircraft had by now been named), SR661, flew for the first time on February 21, 1945, powered by the Centaurus XII. Only semi-navalised, it was

followed in October by a fully navalised aircraft with power-operated folding wings and powered by a Centaurus XV driving a five-bladed propeller.

The end of the war saw the cancellation of the RAF Fury programme and attention was focused on the naval aircraft. Following protracted trials aboard HMS *Victorious* during the winter of 1946-47, the first of 50 production Sea Fury Mk Xs (later designated F.10s) were delivered to 807 Squadron in August 1947.

At the same time Hawker at Langley had been continuously improving the weapon-carrying capability of the aircraft, resulting in a new version designated FB.11. When production finished at the end of 1952 a total of 615 FB.11s had been delivered to the Fleet Air Arm from the Kingston factory. First to receive its FB.11s was

802 Squadron, which formed at Eglinton in May 1948. Four other squadrons, Nos 801, 804, 805 and 807, quickly followed suit, embarking in the light fleet carriers HMS *Ocean, Theseus* and *Glory* from 1949.

The timing could not have been better. The outbreak of the Korean War in 1950 found the Royal Navy equipped with an extremely useful ground-attack aircraft. Starting with 807 Squadron in *Theseus,* the FAA was soon involved in flying support missions for United Nations forces, using bombs and rockets. *Ocean* and *Glory* followed a few months later and, together with Australian and Canadian squadrons, flew thousands of sorties.

Although not as fast as the jet-powered MiG-15s used by the communist forces, Sea Furies nonetheless achieved a number of kills against these

superior aircraft, the first of which was claimed by Lt P. Carmichael of 802 Squadron on April 9, 1952.

From 1953 the Sea Fury began to be superseded in front-line squadrons by the jet-powered Sea Hawk and the type was relegated to use with RNVR units (although the first RNVR squadron, No 1832, had been equipped with the FB.11 as early as 1951).

The Royal Navy operated one other variant of the Sea Fury. This was the two-seat dual-control T.20, the first of which, VX808, flew for the first time on January 15, 1948.

A total of 60 were built for the Fleet Air Arm, with deliveries continuing from mid-1950 until March 1952. They were not equipped for carrier operations and were issued only to RNVR squadrons and Royal Navy training units.

Sea Fury T.20 VX289

Sea Vampire T.22s of 736 Squadron, based at RNAS Lossiemouth

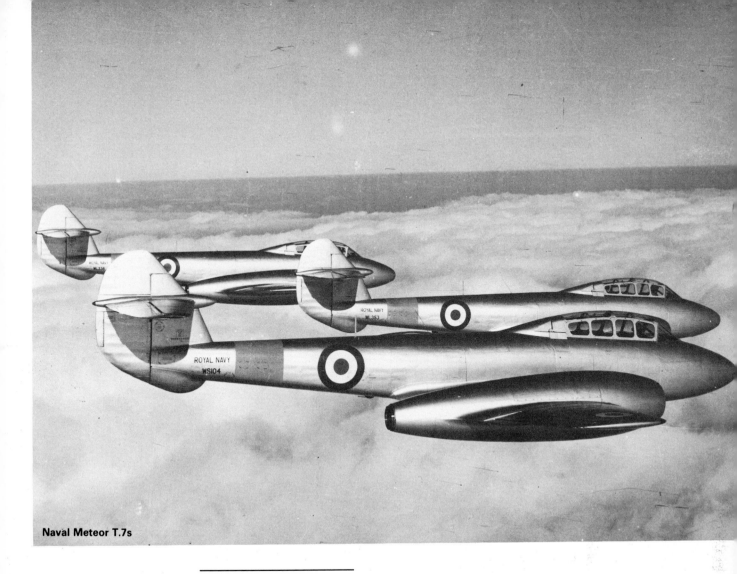

Naval Meteor T.7s

Gloster Meteor T.7

The Meteor T.7 two-seat dual-control trainer was essentially similar to the RAF's F.4 with the exception of the front fuselage. It was powered by two 3,600lb st Rolls-Royce Derwent 5 or 8.

The first production aircraft was flown for the first time in October 1948 and the type entered service initially with the RAF. The Royal Navy acquired a small number for jet training. These aircraft were intended for

shore-based operation only and were not fitted with deck arrester gear or wing-folding facilities.

Two FAA units—Nos 759 and 728 Squadrons—were equipped with the Meteor T.7.

de Havilland Sea Vampire

The Royal Navy's Sea Vampire was a navalised version of the clipped-wing Vampire FB.5 used by the RAF, suitably strengthened for carrier use.

In December 1945 the Vampire became the first pure-jet aircraft to operate from the deck of an aircraft carrier. First flight of the production Sea Vampire F.20 was made in October 1948. Only 18 aircraft

were built and these were used for familiarising Navy aircrew with jet aircraft during 1949 and 1950.

One of the more bizarre exploits of this twin-boom aircraft was a series of deck-landing trials in early 1949 without the benefit of an undercarriage. HMS *Warrior,* the ship chosen to test this novel method of recovering aircraft,

was fitted with a rubberised deck, while the aircraft themselves had their undersides strengthened.

Only three FAA units—the second-line Nos 700, 702 and 787 Squadrons—were equipped with the Sea Vampire.

The Royal Navy also had a number of two-seat Vampire T.22 trainers. A total of 74 were built during 1954 and 1955.

Hiller HTE-2

The emergence of a significant helicopter component in the Fleet Air Arm in the years immediately following the Second World War rapidly resulted in a requirement for a suitable training machine.

First to be acquired was the Hiller HTE-2, a version of the American UH-12. The type was first flown in the USA in 1948, and some 20 were supplied to the Royal Navy in 1950 under MDAP arrangements. Most were used by 705 Squadron. Powerplant was the 200 hp Franklin 6V4-200.

One of those delivered, XB516, was fitted with pontoon floats and operated from the 2,000-ton survey ship HMS *Vidal*.

Royal Navy HTE-2s were superseded by the more advanced Hiller HT-2 in 1963.

Hunting Percival Sea Prince

The Royal Navy used three variants of the twin-engined P.57 Sea Prince: the C.1 and C.2 for communications and VIP transport, and the T.1 for navigation and anti-submarine observer training.

The original P.50 Prince flew for the first time at Luton on May 13, 1948, powered by two 500 hp Alvis Leonides 14 radial engines. Both the Royal Navy and the RAF used versions of the aircraft, but the naval version emerged first, with the first Sea Prince C.1, WF136, making its first flight on March 24, 1950. Fitted out for special communications work, it was followed by a further three C.1s, one of which was configured as an "Admiral's Barge" VIP transport.

The T.1 version which followed featured a lengthened nose to house radar equipment and was fitted out to carry three students together with the special radar and radio equipment needed for its training role. The first T.1 made its first flight on June 28, 1951, at Luton; a total of 42 were built.

Final production variant was the C.2, a communications version of the long-nosed T.1. Three were completed, the first flying for the first time on April 1, 1953.

Sea Prince T.1 from Lossiemouth

Short Sturgeon TT.2: ugly but efficient

Short Sturgeon

The outstandingly ugly Sturgeon was a high-speed twin-engined target tug which started life as a reconnaissance bomber. Built to Specification S.11/43, the prototype, RK787, was flown for the first time by Geoffrey Tyson on June 7, 1946, at Rochester. Shortly after this event, however, the original strike specification was cancelled and the Sturgeon metamorphosed first into a high-speed photo-reconnaissance aircraft carrying a crew of two and a generous helping of cameras, before finally assuming the more mundane guise of specialised target tug to Specification Q.1/46.

Two prototypes of the new

Sturgeon TT.2, VR363 and VR371, were built, and the first of these flew for the first time on September 1, 1949. Fully navalised with folding wings and deck arrester gear, some 24 of this initial mark were completed, all powered by a pair of 1,660 hp Rolls-Royce Merlin 140S engines driving wicked-looking six-bladed contra-rotating propellers.

From the time of their service acceptance in February 1950 the TT.2s were used in small numbers from fleet carriers by the shore-based fleet requirements unit and No 728 Squadron based at Hal Far, Malta.

When the Royal Navy

discontinued "throw off" target practice a number of TT.2s were converted, from November 1953, to TT.3 standard by the removal of deck landing aids and the deletion of the nose-mounted camera. Nine were scheduled for conversion but only five in fact underwent this piece of surgery, and these continued to serve at Hal Far until as late as 1957.

The Sturgeon suffered one further indignity which mercifully did not result in the creation of a production aircraft. This was the creation of the prototype SB.3, a Sturgeon altered to meet the requirements of Specification M.6/49 calling for an

anti-submarine search and patrol aircraft (which ultimately appeared in the form of the Fairey Gannet).

The only SB.3 built, SH1599, first flew on August 12, 1950, powered by two 1,475 shp Armstrong Siddeley Mamba turboprops. The front fuselage of this unhappy aircraft was drastically modified to accommodate two radar operators in a cabin ahead of the pilot's cockpit, while a grotesque chin radome concealed the search radar scanner. Difficult handling, amongst other shortcomings, resulted in the programme being abandoned in early 1951.

Westland Dragonfly

In 1947 Westland acquired a licence to build the Sikorsky S-51 two-seat helicopter. Both the RAF and the Royal Navy received military versions of this aircraft under the designation Dragonfly.

First production version for the Navy was the Dragonfly HR.1 powered by a 550 hp Alvis Leonides 50 radial engine. This was intended for the utility and SAR roles, and a total of 13 were built. In addition to operation from RN ships and shore bases, the Dragonfly was used early in 1951 in a series of experiments designed to test its suitability for operation from the decks of merchant ships.

The main production variant for the Royal Navy was the HR.3, some 50 of which were built. Final naval Dragonfly was the HR.5, only nine of which were completed.

Used extensively for plane-guard duties during carrier flying in the 1950s, the Dragonfly was withdrawn from use with the gradual introduction of the Westland Whirlwind.

Westland WS-51 Dragonfly, the Royal Navy's first "plane-guard" helicopter

Dragonfly HR.3s and two Whirlwinds from HMS *Ocean*

Attacker F.1 WA469 shows its uncluttered lines

Attacker FB.1 with auxiliary ventral fuel tank photographed in August 1952

Supermarine Attacker

The Attacker single-seat carrierborne fighter was significant in being the Royal Navy's first-ever front-line jet fighter. It had its origins in Joe Smith's laminar-wing Spitfire development, the superlative Spiteful, which had been designed for the RAF to Specification F.1/43.

Work during 1944 on the then-new Rolls-Royce Nene axial-flow turbojet resulted in the drafting of Specification E.10/44 for a single-engined fighter to take advantage of this potentially war-winning engine. Supermarine's answer was to mate the Spiteful's wing, complete with landing gear, to a new fuselage housing the 5,000lb st engine.

Designated Supermarine Type 392, the first prototype, TS409, was flown for the first time at Chilbolton by Jeffrey Quill on July 27, 1946. With the RAF showing no interest in the type, the second and third prototypes were built to meet the naval requirements of Specification E.1/45 and were fitted with long-stroke undercarriages, spoilers and deck arrester gear. The first to this standard, TS413, was designated Supermarine Type 398 and first flew in June 1947. First production contract for the new aircraft, now named the Attacker, was placed in November 1949 and the first of these, WA496, flew on April 5, 1950. When production ended in 1953 a total of 145 had been completed for the Fleet Air Arm.

Three versions of the Attacker were built: the F.1, FB.1 and FB.2. The F.1, which first entered service with 800 Squadron at Ford in August 1951, was powered by the 5,100lb st Nene 3, as was the FB.1. The FB.2 was powered by the Nene 102 and featured modified ailerons and a revised cockpit hood. Later FB.2s also had a dorsal fin extension, but all Attackers kept the curiously anachronistic tailwheel undercarriage, which caused more operating problems with runway erosion and the like than officialdom cared to admit to. Like the FB.1, the FB.2 was equipped with underwing stores racks for two 1,000lb bombs or 16 rockets.

By 1953 Attackers equipped three front-line squadrons, Nos 800, 803 and 890, as well as 736 Squadron, a training unit. When Sea Hawks and Sea Venoms superseded them in 1954 the Attackers were passed on to RNVR squadrons, which continued to operate them until 1957.

Attacker FB.2 of 800 Squadron tangled up in *Eagle*'s barrier

Firefly AS.7 WJ149, last of the marque

Fairey Firefly AS.7

The Firefly AS.7 was a three-seat unarmed anti-submarine search aircraft that was intended as an interim step, in company with the Grumman Avenger AS.4, pending service entry of the Fairey Gannet.

Powered by a 1,965 hp Rolls-Royce Griffon 59 engine driving a four-bladed propeller, this variant had the original "beard" radiator. Other major airframe changes were revised wing planform and a substantially larger tail fin. Operational equipment included radar and radio equipment for receiving sonobuoy transmissions.

The prototype AS.7, WJ215, flew for the first time on May 22, 1951, and the first production example in the following October. In addition to the AS.7, production also included a small number of T.7s intended for training observers. A total of 151 Mk 7s were completed, the last in December 1953.

First operational unit to be equipped was 824 Squadron, which retained its AS.7s until re-equipped with Gannets in February 1955. Only one other front-line squadron, No 814, was equipped with the AS.7. The remainder of the Mk 7s were used as trainers by Nos 719, 737, 744, 750, 756, 765 and 766 Squadrons.

Westland Wyvern

The huge turboprop Wyvern, Westland's mythical winged dragon, was to remain a controversial aircraft throughout its life. With its greatly protracted development period and occasionally stormy operational career, the type has a rare ability to polarise opinion amongst those who flew and maintained it and those who would later document it. All were agreed, however, that there had never been anything quite like it.

The Wyvern was originally designed to Specification N.11/44, which called for a long-range carrier/land-based strike fighter. Although the concept of turboprop powerplants had been formulated when the specification was first drawn up, none was thought likely to be available in the timescale originally set out for the Wyvern, and the massive 24-cylinder, 2,690 hp Rolls-Royce Eagle was chosen to power the new fighter.

Six Eagle-powered prototypes, designated Westland Type W.34, were ordered in November 1944. At about the same time the RAF evinced some interest in the project to fill its Specification F.13/44, but this was dropped in December 1945.

The prototype Wyvern I (TS371), as the W.34 was now called, flew for the first time at Boscombe Down on December 12, 1946. Neither this aircraft nor the second prototype to fly, TS375, was navalised, but the third and subsequent prototypes featured fully folding wings, arrester gear and a new six-bladed contra-rotating

Eagle-engined Wyvern TF.1 at Yeovil

Wyvern S.4s

Immaculate formation flying by Wyvern S.4s

Wyvern S.4s of 813 Squadron with unusually painted ventral tanks

propeller.

In August 1946 a contract was placed for 20 production Wyvern TF.1s, to be powered by the Rolls-Royce Eagle. Cancellation of that engine programme in December resulted in the contract being halved, and the ten TF.1s completed were used exclusively for handling trials.

By this time both the Rolls-Royce Clyde and the Armstrong Siddeley Python turboprops were in prospect, and three additional Wyvern prototypes were ordered to Specification N.12/45. The first TF.2, VP120, flew for the first time on January 18, 1949,

powered by the 4,050 ehp Clyde. The Python, however, was to be the definitive powerplant and the first Wyvern powered by this engine, VP109, flew for the first time in March that year.

But it was to be a further four years before the first operational Wyvern S.4s entered service with the Fleet Air Arm, for that is how long it took to get the engine/airframe combination up to an acceptable level of safety.

The first S.4s entered service with 813 Squadron at Ford from May 1953, replacing the squadron's Firebrands. These early production aircraft remained land-based until cleared for deck operations the

following year, when 813 Squadron embarked in HMS *Albion* to exercise in the Mediterranean.

The second front-line Wyvern squadron to form was No 827, which embarked in HMS *Eagle* in May 1955 in company with 813 Squadron, exercising again in the Mediterranean. Both squadrons returned to Ford to disband in November.

Almost simultaneously the final two Wyvern squadrons, Nos 830 and 831, formed at Ford with new aircraft. Both were to have joined *Eagle* in the following year for a Mediterranean cruise, but in fact only 830 Squadron remained on

board. It was thus the only Wyvern unit to be used operationally, in the Anglo-French adventure against Egypt during the Suez crisis in October 1956.

The type was eventually withdrawn from service in March 1958, when 813 Squadron, which had reformed in November 1956, finally disbanded.

Westland built some 127 Wyverns, of which 87 were S.4s. No fewer than 27 S.4s were lost or damaged beyond repair, in addition to the total of ten earlier versions destroyed in the lengthy development period.

Whirlwind HAS.7 with dunking sonar

Westland/Sikorsky Whirlwind

The first Whirlwind helicopters to be used by the Royal Navy were built by Sikorsky in the USA as the S-55 and supplied to Britain under MDAP contracts.

The prototype S-55 first flew on November 7, 1949, powered by a 550 hp Pratt & Whitney R-1340-S1H2 radial engine. About 25 were acquired by the Fleet Air Arm in two versions: the HAR.21, which was the equivalent of the US Marines' HRS-2, and the HAS.22, powered by the 700 hp Wright Cyclone R-1300-3 and equivalent to the US Navy's HO4S-3.

First to enter squadron service was the HAR.21, with 848 Squadron, which was formed to carry out utility and transport duties. The Fleet Air Arm's first helicopter anti-submarine squadron was No 845, equipped with the HAS.22, which began operations in the spring of 1954.

Later, when they had been replaced by more modern types, some HAS.22s were used on general communications duties by 781 Squadron at Lee-on-Solent and remained in service with this unit until as late as 1969.

Westland acquired manufacturing rights to the S-55 in 1950. The first version to be built for the Royal Navy by the British manufacturer was the HAR.1, the prototype of which (XA862) first flew on August 15, 1953. Only ten production aircraft were completed and these served with 705 Squadron.

The next Westland-built version for the Navy was the HAR.3, which, like the Sikorsky-built HAS.22, was powered by a 700 hp Wright Cyclone engine. A total of 20 production HAR.3s were

completed.

Availability of a British engine in the form of the 750 hp Alvis Leonides Major Mk 155 resulted in the Whirlwind HAR.5. The prototype, XJ396, first flew on August 28, 1955, but only seven were built. Airframe changes included a modified tailcone and rear pylon and a new horizontal stabiliser.

The HAR.1, 3 and 5 had all been equipped for search and rescue and communications roles, but the HAS.7 which followed was specifically designed for anti-submarine operations and was accordingly equipped with radar, dipping sonar and facilities for carrying a homing torpedo.

The prototype HAS.7, XG589, flew for the first time on October 17, 1956, and first deliveries of production aircraft were made to the Helicopter Flight of 700

Squadron in June 1957. The first operational unit was 845 Squadron, which received the first of its new Whirlwinds in August that year. A total of 120 were completed and a substantial number of surviving Mk 7s were converted to the commando troop-carrying role from May 1963, serving with Nos 846 and 847 Squadrons. The last was withdrawn from service in August 1975.

A number of Mk 7s were also converted to HAR.9 standard for search and rescue duties. The conversion principally comprised the fitting of a 1,050 shp Bristol Siddeley Gnome turboshaft engine in place of the old Leonides radial. They were based at the RNAS stations at Brawdy, Culdrose and Lee-on-Solent from the middle of 1966 and were replaced by Wessex 5s from the summer of 1975.

Whirlwind HAR.9 from HMS *Endurance*

Pair of Sea Balliols of JOAC, the Junior Officers' Air Course

Boulton Paul Sea Balliol T.21

Originally produced to meet Specification T.7/45 for a three-seat turboprop trainer for the RAF, the Balliol in its definitive form was a two-seat side-by-side aircraft powered by a 1,280 hp Rolls-Royce Merlin 35.

The first of these aircraft flew for the first time on July 10, 1948, and equipped RAF flying schools from 1950.

The Royal Navy requested a version for training regular and RNVR pilots in deck handling techniques. Designated Sea Balliol T.21, the first prototype made its first flight in October 1952. Total production amounted to 30, the last of which was delivered in December 1954.

Seamew XA213 was one of two prototypes

Short Seamew

By the end of the Second World War the importance of anti-submarine warfare had been fully appreciated by the Allied forces, and within the Admiralty most agreed on the value of aircraft in that role. There was growing concern, however, at the increasing cost and complexity of such aircraft, and an attempt was made to reverse this trend with the issuing in 1951 of Specification M.123 for a simple, lightweight ASW aircraft suitable for operation from the smaller aircraft carriers.

Best of the designs tendered was the Short SB.6. Powered by an Armstrong Siddeley Mamba turboprop, it was an awkward-looking aeroplane with fixed undercarriage and a crew of two perched high up and well forward in the deep fuselage.

Three prototypes were ordered (XA209, 213 and 216) in April 1952 and the first of these was flown for the first time at Sydenham in August 1953. Designed only to loiter on long reconnaissance patrols, it was not blessed with sparkling performance and the handling of the prototype was also quite seriously deficient in many respects. Nevertheless, a production order for 41 aircraft was placed in February 1955 (some of which were earmarked for RAF Coastal Command). Meanwhile, a number of aerodynamic refinements having been made, XA213 underwent carrier trials on board HMS *Bulwark* during the summer of 1955.

Deliveries of the definitive production aircraft, with their distinctive bulged radomes, began in 1956, but shortly afterwards the RAF order was cancelled and the order reduced to only 24 Seamew AS.1s for the Royal Navy. Trials at RNAS Lossiemouth continued until the programme was cancelled in its entirety as part of the notorious 1957 defence cutback.

Although it entered production, the Seamew never saw front-line service

Sea Hawks from HMS *Eagle* fire their starter cartridges in unison

Sea Hawk FGA.4s of 898 Squadron, from HMS *Eagle*'s air group

Hawker Sea Hawk

The Sea Hawk was a single-seat carrierborne ground-attack fighter which lies in Fleet Air Arm history between the first-generation jet Attacker and the nuclear-capable Scimitar.

Like most British military aircraft of the mid-1950s, the Sea Hawk originated in a proposal drafted during the later stages of the Second World War. In this particular case it was the Hawker P.1040 project, built around the new Rolls-Royce B.41 jet engine. Although it elicited no interest from the RAF, the Naval Staff was sufficiently impressed by the design's potential as a future fleet support fighter to order three prototypes to Specification N.7/46.

The P.1040 prototype, VP401, flew for the first time at Boscombe Down on September 2, 1947, but lacked the operational and naval equipment of the first truly naval prototype, VP413, which first flew almost exactly one year later. This aircraft featured folding wings, catapult points and arrester gear, and gun armament consisting of four nose-mounted Hispano 20mm

800 Squadron's Sea Hawks pull up for a formation loop

cannon.

The first production contract, for 151 Sea Hawk F.1s, was placed in November 1949 and production was begun at Kingston. After 35 Sea Hawks had been completed the line was transferred to Armstrong Whitworth at Coventry to make room for Hunter production. The first production F.1 flew in November 1951 but the type did not enter service, with 806

Squadron at RNAS Brawdy, until March 1953.

Next version to be built was the F.2, which incorporated power-assisted ailerons. Armstrong Whitworth built 40 during 1954, the first flying for the first time on February 24. Also built at Coventry during 1954 were 116 FB.3s with wings strengthened for extra load-carrying. The FB.3s were followed by 97 close-support

FGA.4s, the first of which made its first flight in August. Five front-line squadrons were equipped: Nos 803, 804, 810, 897 and 898. Retrofitting the Navy's FB.3s and FGA.4s with the uprated Nene 103 engine produced the FB.5 and FGA.6, respectively, but little increase in performance.

About 50 FB.3s and a handful of FGA.4s were modified and most of the FGA.6s were built

from new, some 87 being delivered between March 1955 and January 1956.

The Sea Hawk first went to sea aboard HMS *Eagle* with 806 Squadron in February 1954 and the type served in front-line squadrons continuously until December 1960. After this the Sea Hawk was used in second-line and training units until the last was withdrawn from use in early 1969.

Douglas Skyraider

The Skyraider was designed in the US during 1944 by the celebrated Ed Heinemann as a replacement for the Dauntless dive bomber. First flown in March 1945, the Skyraider reached Britain in November 1951, when the first of 50 supplied under the Mutual Defence Assistance Programme arrived at Glasgow.

Royal Navy Skyraiders were three-seat carrierborne radar pickets and carried the designation AEW.1. Powered by a 2,700 hp Wright Cyclone engine, the Skyraider had a formidable load-carrying ability; this was fortunate, since the AN/APS-20A radar carried in the large ventral radome weighed about a ton.

Initial trials of the aircraft and its electronics equipment were carried out by 778 Squadron based at RNAS Culdrose in Cornwall. Formed on October 1, 1951, the squadron was redesignated as a front-line unit and renumbered 849 Squadron in July 1952.

By the end of September 1953 sufficient aircraft had arrived in Britain to permit the formation of five flights (A, B, C, D and E) in addition to a headquarters flight. In July 1954, however, this arrangement was rationalised as follows: HQ, A and B Flights with six aircraft each, and C and E Flights with four aircraft each. On its return from Malta in October 1954 E Flight was re-lettered D Flight.

Final deliveries of Skyraiders did not take place until 1956, but spares were a continual problem and by 1958 a number of aircraft had to be cannibalised at RNAS Donibristle to keep the type in operational condition. Most had been retired by early 1961.

Skyraider AEW.1 of 849 Squadron's "A" Flight

Skyraider embarks on a free take-off, to the delight of the "goofers" crowding HMS *Victorious'* superstructure

de Havilland Sea Devon C.20s. XJ324 in the foreground is ex-G-AMXZ

de Havilland Sea Devon and Sea Heron

The Royal Navy acquired a small number of twin-engined Sea Devon C.20s for communications duties. Equivalent to the RAF's Devon, the eight-seat aircraft equipped No 781 Squadron at RNAS Lee-on-Solent from 1955.

Initially ten aircraft were delivered, the majority being ex-civil aircraft; a further three were added to the inventory in January 1956.

In May 1961, with the appearance of the larger four-engined Sea Heron, a number of Sea Devons were returned to civilian life.

Only five Sea Herons were acquired; two were former Jersey Airlines aircraft, while the other three had previously belonged to West African Airways.

The Sea Herons and the remaining Sea Devons were disposed of following the disbandment of 781 Squadron in 1981.

Sea Heron of 781 Squadron

Yeovilton-based Hunter T.8 "Admiral's barge"

Hunter GA.11 advanced trainers of 738 Squadron

Hawker Hunter T.8 and GA.11

The Fleet Air Arm has operated two versions of the Hunter: the two-seat T.8 advanced trainer and the single-seat GA.11 weapons trainer. Like all Hunters they were delightful to fly and excellent in their designated roles.

The dual-control T.8 was the navalised version of the RAF's T.7 and first entered service with 764 Squadron at RNAS Lossiemouth in July 1958. A total of 41 were delivered, 31 of them converted from

single-seat F.4 fighters and the remaining ten being modified T.7s.

When first introduced into the Fleet Air Arm the T.8s were equipped with an Aden cannon and radar ranging, but these features were removed when the aircraft were modified to carry Tacan navigational equipment for their primary role as advanced trainers.

In all, three training squadrons were equipped: Nos

738 and 759 Squadrons at RNAS Brawdy in Wales and No 764 Squadron at RNAS Lossiemouth. In addition, T.8s were made available to operational squadrons for continuation training and a small number were issued as communications aircraft to Flag Officers.

Fleet Air Arm pilots destined for all-weather fighter or strike squadrons graduated from the T.8 to the single-seat GA.11. A

total of 40 were delivered from 1962 and all were converted ex-RAF F.4s.

In 738 Squadron, based at RNAS Brawdy, the GA.11s were used extensively for weapons training. With the running-down of the fixed-wing Fleet Air Arm during the 1970s a number were transferred to the Fleet Requirements and Air Directions Unit (FRADU) at Yeovilton, where they were flown by civilian pilots.

Sea Venom FAW.21 XG612

Sea Venom FAW.21s from 890 Squadron

de Havilland Sea Venom

The Sea Venom was a two-seat carrierborne all-weather and strike fighter developed from the RAF's Venom NF.2 night fighter. Designed to Specification N.107, the first of the true Sea Venom prototypes flew for the first time at Hatfield on April 19, 1951, and carried out its first deck handling trials during July that year from the aircraft carrier HMS *Illustrious*.

Some 50 production aircraft were built, bearing the designation FAW.20, and the last of these was delivered in June 1955. The FAW.20 was powered by the de Havilland Ghost 103, uprated to the Ghost 104 for the FAW.21 version, which also featured power-operated ailerons, revised clear-view cockpit canopy, Martin-Baker Mk 4 ejection seat and a new American AI.21 radar. Total production of the FAW.21 was 166.

Final production version was the FAW.22, powered by the DH Ghost 105. Only 39 were built as new, but several FAW.21s were brought up to the later standard during 1957 and 1958.

Sea Venom FAW.20s first entered service with 703 Squadron at Ford in 1953 before the formation of 890 Squadron, the first operational unit, in February 1954. Second unit to form was 809 Squadron, which, like 890 Squadron, commissioned at RNAS Yeovilton. Last of the three FAW.20 squadrons was No 891, which formed in November 1954.

The FAW.20 had only a brief spell at sea, aboard HMS *Albion*, and a spate of hook failures led to the type being relegated to second-line shore-based duties.

FAW.21s entered service with 809 Squadron in May 1955, and by mid-1956 a further four squadrons—Nos 890, 891, 892 and 893—were similarly equipped. Three of these squadrons took part in the Suez War during the autumn of 1956: 809 Squadron embarked in HMS *Albion* and 892 and 893 Squadrons aboard HMS *Eagle*.

From the middle of 1959 the Sea Venom was progressively replaced in front-line squadrons by the Sea Vixen FAW.1. But the type could be seen operating from Yeovilton with the Fleet Requirements Unit up to October 1970, when the last FAW.22 was withdrawn.

Discarding its catapult strop, a Sea Venom FAW.22 from 894 Squadron takes off

Fairey Gannet (Mks 1, 2, 4 and 5)

The Gannet was the Fairey Aviation Co's last naval aircraft and was designed to perform two roles: anti-submarine search and strike.

Originally designated the Fairey Type Q, the Gannet was the first aircraft in the world to be powered by a double propeller-turbine unit, either half of which could be independently shut down to provide the economies of single-engined operation without the disadvantages of asymmetric handling.

A prototype of the Type Q was ordered in August 1946 to Specification GR.17/45, competing against the unsuccessful Blackburn YB.1. At first the projected Rolls-Royce Tweed was considered to power the Type Q, but the 2,950 ehp Armstrong Siddeley Double Mamba engine (consisting of two 1,010 ehp Mamba ASM.3 turbine engines linked to a common gearbox) was eventually chosen. Running trials of the new engine began during 1948.

The first prototype, VR546, was completed in 1949 and flew for the first time on September 19 that year. Both VR546 and the second prototype, VR557, were initially completed as two-seat aircraft and featured double-folding wings and a large weapons bay, aft of which was situated a retractable "dustbin" radome.

A change in naval requirements led to the provision of a third seat in the next prototype (WE488), and as a consequence the radar antenna had to be moved further aft. Ordered in June 1949, this aircraft flew for the first time on May 10, 1951, and, joined by the first two prototypes, underwent an intensive flying development programme.

Production orders for 100 Gannet AS.1s were placed in March 1951 and the first of these was flown for the first time in June 1953. Total production of the AS.1 eventually totalled 172

Gannet AS.1 with "dustbin" radome extended

WN365, the Gannet T.2 prototype

aircraft.

First unit to be equipped was 703X Flight, the Squadron Service Trials Unit based at Ford, Sussex, in April 1954. The first operational unit to form was 826 Squadron, at RNAS Lee-on-Solent in January 1955. This was followed by Nos 824 and 825 Squadrons.

The requirement for a dual-controlled Gannet trainer led to the development of the T.2, the first of which flew for the first time in August 1954. A total

of 36 were produced, equipping Fleet Air Arm training squadrons from 1955. In addition to the provision of dual controls the T.2s were characterised by the elimination of the ventral radome, the rear radar operator's cockpit being available for either a radio operator or two passengers. The first production model was delivered to 737 Squadron at Eglinton, Northern Ireland, in March 1955.

Next anti-submarine version

to appear was the AS.4, the first of which first flew on April 13, 1956. This version differed from the AS.1 in having the more powerful 3,035 ehp Double Mamba 101 engine. A total of 90 AS.4s were built and these, together with the AS.1s, carried out all of the Fleet Air Arm's anti-submarine operations until supplanted by the Westland Whirlwind helicopter from 1958. All had been withdrawn by the middle of 1960.

Final production variant in the

first series was the T.5, training version of the AS.4. Eight were produced, modified from the last T.2s on the assembly line. The Gannet trainers continued to be used for training AEW.3 crews after the last of the AS series had been withdrawn.

During 1961 a small number of AS.4s were refurbished and fitted with comprehensive radar and electronics equipment. Designated AS.6, they served with 831 Squadron at RNAS Culdrose on ECM duties.

Gannet AS.4

First production Scimitar F.1, XD212

Supermarine Scimitar

Remarkably, the Scimitar was the Fleet Air Arm's first swept-wing fighter, even though it did not enter service until 1957. Part of the delay was due to the protracted development of this single-seat twin-engined aircraft, which began life as the butterfly-tailed Supermarine Type 508, first flown on August 31, 1951. In fact the Type 508 itself had been preceded by a curious undercarriageless project, the Type 505, but for a variety of reasons this programme was terminated and the Admiralty's attention directed towards a more orthodox type of shipborne fighter.

Three Type 508s were ordered to Specification N.9/47. The first, VX133, retained the straight wing of the Type 505, while the second, VX136, emerged with slight revisions as the Type 529. The most dramatic change, however, was wrought on the third prototype, VX138. This became the Type 525 with new swept-back wings and the butterfly tail replaced by a conventional fin-and-rudder assembly. This aircraft flew for the first time on April 27, 1954. By that time, however, Naval Specification N.113D had been drafted and an additional three prototypes ordered. Redesignated Supermarine Type 544, the first of these, WT854, first flew on January 19, 1956, powered by a pair of 11,250lb st Rolls-Royce Avon 202s.

The Scimitar incorporated a number of novel features in its design, amongst them area ruling of the fuselage and the introduction of "blown" flaps to reduce the safe approach speed, particularly for carrier landings, and the catapult speed. It was also the first naval aircraft capable of carrying a nuclear device. In keeping with its primary strike role a number of other weapons could be carried, including 500lb or 1,000lb bombs, 2in or 3in unguided rockets and Bullpup air-to-ground missiles in addition to four 30mm Aden cannon.

A total of 100 Scimitars was ordered, of which 76 were actually delivered. First production aircraft flew in January 1957 and reached No 700X Trials Flight at Ford in August that year. The first operational squadron, No 803, was formed at RNAS Lossiemouth in June 1958, to be followed by Nos 800, 804 and 807 Squadrons.

**807 Squadron's Scimitars
pull up into a formation loop**

Armstrong-Whitworth-built Meteor TT.20

Armstrong Whitworth Meteor TT.20

Developed from the Meteor NF.11, the Meteor TT.20 was produced to satisfy a naval requirement for a high-speed target tug for fleet requirements units.

Work to modify a basic NF.11 began in 1957 and the first TT.20s entered service late the following year with 728 FRU, based at Hal Far on Malta, and at 776 FRU at Hurn.

The TT.20 could carry four high-speed radar-responsive sleeve targets, measuring either 3ft by 15ft or 4ft by 20ft, which were stowed in the modified rear fuselage. A windmill-driven winch was mounted on a streamlined pylon on the starboard wing centre-section to handle the 6,000ft towing cable.

Sea Vixen FAW.1 XJ520 of 766 Squadron

Hawker Siddeley (de Havilland) Sea Vixen FAW.1

The twin-engined two-seat DH.110 Sea Vixen was the largest of the de Havilland twin-boom designs which had originated in the wood-fuselage Vampire.

First proposed in 1946 to meet Naval Specification N.40/46 for an all-weather fighter, the design was also amended to meet Specification F.44/46 for an advanced night fighter for the RAF. Detailed design did not begin until 1948, however, and Specification F.44/46 was replaced by the updated F.4/48. In April 1949 the Ministry of Supply ordered a total of nine prototypes for the RAF and a further four for the Royal Navy. In November, however, the Admiralty cancelled its order in favour of the Sea Venom and the RAF reduced its prototype requirement to just two DH.110s together with two prototypes of the competing Gloster GA.5 (later to enter service with the

Four greens to land: Vixen looking for the third wire

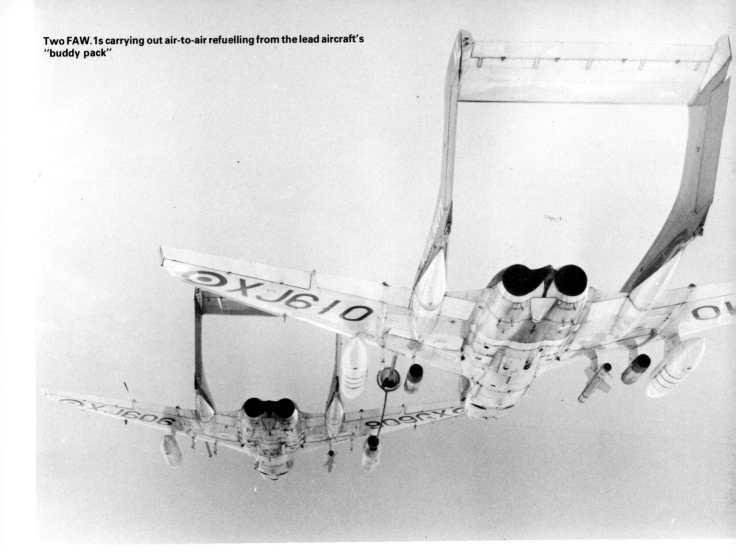

Two FAW.1s carrying out air-to-air refuelling from the lead aircraft's "buddy pack"

RAF as the Javelin).

The first prototype DH.110, WG236, was flown for the first time on September 26, 1951, by John Cunningham. Powered by two 7,500lb st Rolls-Royce Avon RA.7s, it achieved supersonic speed in a shallow dive in the following April. Tragedy struck in September 1952, however, when WG236 broke up in the air at the SBAC show at Farnborough, killing pilot John Derry, his flight test observer Tony Richards and a number of spectators.

The RAF's interest in the DH.110 all but evaporated in 1953 when the GA.5 was ordered into production as the Javelin. But the Royal Navy still had an outstanding need for an advanced all-weather fighter under Specification N.14/49 and it was decided that the design should be reworked to suit the new naval requirements.

The second DH.110 prototype,

WG240, which had first flown in July 1952, went through a succession of structural changes and by the time it began preliminary sea trials on board HMS *Albion* in September 1954 it was beginning to look very much like the definitive Sea Vixen.

In January 1955 a production order was finally issued, to Specification N.139P, and the first of these fully navalised aircraft, XJ474, was rolled out at Christchurch in February 1957 and flown for the first time on March 20. The first contract was for 45 FAW.1s; this was followed by a follow-on order for 39 aircraft in June 1959 and by a final batch of 26 in August 1960.

The first Sea Vixen FAW.1 was delivered to No 700Y Service Trials Unit at RNAS Yeovilton in November 1957. After intensive development flying 700Y was reformed as 892 Squadron, which commissioned in July

1959. After a work-up period the squadron embarked in HMS *Ark Royal* in March 1960, beginning a round of commissions which would take it to the carriers *Victorious, Hermes* and *Centaur* during the next four years.

From 1960 the Sea Vixen progressively replaced the Sea Venoms in FAA all-weather fighter squadrons and, in addition to 892 Squadron, Nos 890, 893 and 899 Squadrons were equipped, while No 766 Squadron provided the Sea Vixen OCU.

The weapon system of the Vixen was respectable for its day, consisting of an AI.18 radar with its scanner enclosed in a vast nose radome, and four Firestreak infra-red homing air-to-air guided missiles or four Microcell rocket packs plus 28 2in rockets stowed in a retractable pack in the fuselage belly. In the strike role it could carry two 1,000lb bombs.

Prototype Gannet AEW.3 XJ440

Fairey Gannet AEW.3

The Gannet AEW.3 was designed to replace the Douglas Skyraider as the Fleet Air Arm's standard airborne early-warning aircraft.

Derived from earlier anti-submarine versions of the Gannet, the AEW.3 introduced an entirely new fuselage and tail assembly, mated to a more powerful version of the Double Mamba engine. Other changes included the fitting of a large ventral radome under the pilot's cockpit to house the ASV radar, and new longer-stroke undercarriage housed in redesigned inner wing panels. Crew accommodation was modified so that instead of enjoying a glazed cockpit each the two radar operators were

enclosed in a cabin in the rear fuselage.

The first prototype, XJ440, flew for the first time at Northolt on August 20, 1958, and, without radar and other operational equipment, began handling trials aboard HMS *Centaur* in November. The first production aircraft, XL449, flew the following month.

No 700G Intensive Trials Flight was set up at Culdrose in the summer of 1959 and type proving had been completed by the end of January 1960, when the unit was designated 849 Squadron "A" Flight.

The AEW.3 served only with 849 Squadron during its career, and the squadron's four flights served at one time or another

aboard five of the Royal Navy's aircraft carriers ("A" and "B" Flights in *Victorious;* "B" Flight in *Centaur;* "B" and "C" Flights in *Ark Royal;* "D" Flight in *Eagle;* and "A," "B" and "C" Flights in *Hermes).*

The Headquarters Flight, meanwhile, was located first at RNAS Culdrose before moving to RNAS Brawdy in December 1974 and finally to RNAS Lossiemouth in November 1970.

A total of 43 production AEW.3s were completed, but such was the wear and tear on these aircraft that only 13 remained operational by 1977. The withdrawal from service of HMS *Ark Royal* in 1979 resulted in the final retirement of the last Gannet AEW.3s.

Gannet 3 lifts off from *Victorious'* angled deck . . .

. . . while another tangles messily with *Ark Royal*'s barrier

Trio of Lossiemouth-based Buccaneer S.1s

Hawker Siddeley (Blackburn) Buccaneer S.1

The Buccaneer was intended as a high-speed, low-level strike aircraft to replace the Wyvern in Fleet Air Arm squadrons. The original specification, M.148T (or NA.39), was issued in 1952 and Blackburn's tender, for an aircraft conceived under the design leadership of B.P. Laight, was accepted in July 1955. A Ministry of Supply order for 20 pre-production aircraft followed.

The time between the beginning of detailed design work and completion of the first prototype, XK486, was commendably short. The newly completed aircraft was taken by road from Blackburn's factory at Brough to the RAE at Bedford for a first flight on April 30, 1958.

The Buccaneer incorporated a number of novel features, including generous area ruling of the fuselage, and "supercirculation" boundary-layer control, which helped maintain the effectiveness of the wing flaps and drooped ailerons at the low airspeed desirable for carrier approaches and landings. The boundary-layer air came from the final compressor stage of the aircraft's two 7,100lb st Gyron Junior turbojets. Also noteworthy was the rotating bomb bay in the aircraft's belly, which could accommodate a tactical nuclear weapon.

Development test flying by the pre-production aircraft continued through to the delivery in March 1961 of six aircraft to No 700Z Flight, the Intensive Flying Trials Unit at RNAS Lossiemouth.

The first operational unit to be equipped was 801 Squadron, which commissioned at Lossiemouth on July 17, 1962, and embarked in HMS *Ark Royal* in the English Channel in the following February. A few months later, however, 801 Squadron removed itself to HMS *Victorious*, which relieved HMS *Centaur* off the coast of East Africa in early 1964 to continue the Beira oil patrol precipitated by the declaration of UDI by Rhodesia.

Two other front-line squadrons were equipped with the Buccaneer S.1: No 809 Squadron, which commissioned in January 1963, and No 800 Squadron, which commissioned in March 1964. No 809 was the HQ squadron and eventually re-formed as 736 Squadron, the Buccaneer OCU.

From 1965 the S.1 was superseded in front-line squadrons by the more advanced Spey-engined S.2.

Buccaneer S.1 XK534, one of the pre-production batch

Wessex Mk 1 configured as an anti-submarine aircraft

Wessex Mk 1 operating as a commando transport

Westland Wessex HAS.1 and HAS.3

The Wessex HAS.1 was the first of the Wessex variants to be built for the Royal Navy. Based on the Sikorsky S-58 airframe, the Westland-built version was significant in being the first helicopter in quantity production to use a free-turbine powerplant.

The prototype Wessex, XL722, was an imported Sikorsky HSS-1 re-engined with a 1,450 shp Napier Gazelle gas turbine. It flew for the first time on May 17, 1957. The first Westland-built example, XL727, first flew on June 20, 1958.

Intended from the outset as an anti-submarine helicopter to replace the Whirlwind, the Wessex HAS.1 was equipped with Doppler radar, an advanced autostabilisation system and various externally carried weapons such as two homing torpedoes. The Wessex could also be used for search and rescue operations or troop transport, and in the latter role it could accommodate up to 16 fully equipped troops.

The Wessex HAS.3 was a pure anti-submarine variant

After service trials with No 700H Flight at RNAS Culdrose from April 1960 the HAS.1 entered service with 815 Squadron, which commissioned at Culdrose on July 4, 1961. Total production of the HAS.1 amounted to 129 aircraft.

The following year a number of Wessex 1s were converted from anti-submarine to commando assault configuration for operation by No 845 Squadron.

The Wessex HAS.3 was similar to the Mk 1 but was fitted with a 1,600 shp Gazelle Mk 165 engine and a new search radar housed in a dorsal radome aft of the rotor head. In addition, a much more advanced flight control system was installed to enable all phases of an anti-submarine search and strike mission to be performed automatically.

Most of the 50 HAS.3s acquired by the Royal Navy were converted HAS.1s, and they began to enter service with 814 Squadron from the end of 1966. With the introduction of the Westland Sea King HAS.1 in 1970 the Wessex was relegated to the training role.

Hiller HT.2

When the Hiller HTE-2 was withdrawn from service in 1963 the Royal Navy replaced these training helicopters with 14 examples of the more advanced HT.2.

Powered by a 305 hp Lycoming VO-540-A1B piston engine, the HT.2 was equivalent to the Hiller 12E, designated OH-23G in the US Army.

The Fleet Air Arm later acquired a further seven to bring 705 Squadron's complement to 21. With the introduction of the Westland/Aérospatiale Gazelle for the primary training role the last of the HT.2s was withdrawn from service in March 1975.

Culdrose-based Hiller HT.2, successor to the HTE-2

Wessex HU.5 XT764

Westland Wessex HU.5

The Wessex HU.5 differed from earlier versions of the helicopter principally in being fitted with two coupled 1,350 shp Bristol Siddeley Gnome 110/111 turboshaft engines.

Produced as a troop transport for the Royal Marines, it could carry up to 16 fully equipped troops in addition to its crew. The HU.5 could also carry large external loads such as vehicles, artillery or bulk stores and release them from the hover, and could act as a helicopter gunship.

Construction of the prototype, XS241, began in May 1962, leading to a first flight on May 31, 1963. Production contracts for a total of 100 HU.5s were placed in August 1962 and June 1964, and the first six were delivered to No 700V Intensive Flying Trials Unit at RNAS Culdrose in December 1963.

In addition to two training squadrons, Nos 707 and 772, the HU.5 equipped some four front-line squadrons—Nos 845, 846, 847 and 848—with the first of these embarking in the commando carrier HMS *Bulwark* in 1967.

Wessex HU.5s from HMS *Albion* **disgorge Royal Marine commandos during a Yeovilton air day**

Sea Vixen FAW.2 XP924 was built from new to that standard . . .

Hawker Siddeley Sea Vixen FAW.2

By the time the Sea Vixen FAW.1 entered service it had long been recognised that not only was there stretch potential in the aircraft, but it was one day going to be an operational necessity to improve both its performance and its weapons capability. Various proposals had been put forward in the early years, including the fitting of uprated engines such as the Rolls-Royce Spey, and even replacing the generously sectioned transonic wing with a new one of thinner

section to provide a maximum speed as high as Mach 1.4.

In the event the updating was relatively modest, consisting of installing additional fuel tanks in forward extensions to the tail booms and uprating the armament to include Red Top IR missiles in place of the Firestreaks.

Two FAW.1s were modified to this standard and flew during the summer of 1962. Full-scale

production began at Hawarden in the same year, the first 14 of 29 aircraft having been started as FAW.1s and completed as Mk 2s. The last was completed in 1966. In addition, between 1963 and 1968 no fewer than 67 aircraft were converted from FAW.1 to FAW.2 standard.

First to be equipped was 899 Squadron at RNAS Yeovilton in December 1963. This unit embarked in HMS *Eagle* at the end of 1964, taking part in the

blockade of Rhodesia. Three other front-line squadrons were equipped: Nos 890, 892 and 893 Squadrons. As with the FAW.1, the Vixen 2 OCU was 766 Squadron at Yeovilton.

The FAW.2 left front-line service with the disbanding of 899 Squadron in 1972 and most of the aircraft were scrapped. But a handful were retained by the Fleet Requirements Unit at Yeovilton, while others continue to be used as live missile targets.

. . . while XN653 was a converted FAW.1

XP921 was a Vixen from 899 Squadron

Culdrose-based Westland Wasp HAS.1 with twin Mk 44 homing torpedoes beneath its fuselage

Culdrose-based Westland Wasp HAS.1 with twin Mk 44 homing torpedoes beneath its fuselage

Wasp HAS.1 from the frigate HMS *Leander*

Westland Wasp

The Wasp light anti-submarine helicopter was a direct development of the British Army's Scout and was the first helicopter in Fleet Air Arm service to be deployed extensively throughout the Royal Navy's frigate fleet.

The type originated in the Saunders-Roe P.531 project, the first prototype of which flew for the first time on July 20, 1958. The prototype of the production

version, designated P.531-2 Mk 1, flew for the first time in August 1959, powered by a Rolls-Royce Nimbus gas turbine.

Royal Navy aircraft differed from their Army counterparts in having a folding tail and special undercarriage consisting of four castoring wheels for deck operations. Powerplant was a 710 shp Nimbus 503. The first of 98 production Wasps flew for

the first time on October 28, 1962, with deliveries beginning during the first half of the following year.

First unit to be equipped was 700H Flight, the Intensive Flying Trials Unit, which formed at RNAS Culdrose in the summer of 1963. Headquarters squadron for all Small Ships Flights was 829 Squadron, which commissioned at Culdrose in March 1964, moving to RNAS

Portland in November that year.

In the anti-submarine role the Wasp could carry two Mk 44 homing torpedoes; from 1968 armament was augmented to include the Aérospatiale AS.12M air-to-surface missile.

With the introduction of the Lynx in 1977 Small Ships Flight Wasps were progressively withdrawn from service and relegated to training duties.

Buccaneer S.2s from 700 B Flight, the Intensive Flying Trials Unit, in 1965

Hawker Siddeley Buccaneer S.2

The Buccaneer S.1 had many operational shortcomings, most of which were associated with the Bristol Siddeley Gyron Junior turbojets. With the delivery of the last S.1 from Brough in December 1963, therefore, Hawker Siddeley began preparations for production of the Spey-engined S.2, which would provide the Royal Navy strike squadrons with a much needed increase in capability.

The main airframe modification was the enlargement of the air intakes to cope with the Spey's greater mass flow, and modification of the boundary-layer slits to provide blowing to the inner wing panels, a facility not available on the S.1. The Spey itself provided 30 per cent more thrust, together with a substantially lower specific fuel consumption.

Plans for the developed version were revealed in May 1961 and a production order was placed in the following January (before even the S.1 had entered squadron service).

The first pre-production aircraft (XK526, converted from S.1 standard) flew for the first time on May 17, 1963, and the first full production-standard aircraft, XN974, flew for the first time in the following June. Production ended in December 1968 after 84 aircraft had been completed.

A great deal of development flying was undertaken before the type entered squadron

service in March 1965, including deck operating trials from HMS *Ark Royal* and ''hot and high'' trials in the USA.

The first aircraft were delivered to No 700B Flight, the Buccaneer Intensive Flying Trials Unit, in March 1965. The first operational unit to be commissioned was 801 Squadron, at RNAS Lossiemouth, in October that

year. The squadron embarked in HMS *Victorious* for its first cruise with the new aircraft in June 1966, by which time the second S.2 unit, No 809, had been commissioned (in January 1966). Two other front-line squadrons were formed: No 800 in late 1966 and No 803 in 1967.

In March 1967 the Buccaneer S.2 entered the limelight when aircraft from 800 and 736

Squadrons were called in to destroy the oil tanker *Torrey Canyon,* which had run aground on the Seven Stones Reef off Land's End.

With the running-down of the fixed-wing Fleet Air Arm during the 1970s all of the Navy's S.2s were taken over by the RAF. The first four were delivered to 12 Squadron at RAF Honington as early as October 1969.

An 800 Squadron S.2 on HMS *Eagle*'s catapult

McDonnell Douglas Phantom

The acquisition by the Royal Navy of the outstanding multi-mission Phantom should have been a straightforward great leap forward into the supersonic age. But bureaucratic and political indecision threatened at times to rob the Fleet Air Arm of just about the only strike fighter capable of carrying the current generation of weapons to the enemy over any meaningful distance.

Ordered in February 1964, the first Phantom FG.1s did not enter operational service with the Royal Navy until five years later, in March 1969. The original order was to have been for 140 aircraft but, true to form, the politicians succeeded in whittling this figure down to 28 aircraft, enough for just one squadron.

To its credit, the Royal Navy made excellent use of this small force of Phantoms, and by the time that the engineering difficulties attendant upon fitting the British Spey engine into the American airframe had

been resolved, the result was a fighting machine superior in several respects to the original article.

The first Royal Navy Phantom, XT595, flew for the first time at St Louis on June 27, 1966, carrying the US designation YF-4K. The first production FG.1s arrived at Yeovilton at the end of April 1968 to equip the trials squadron, No 700P. The Phantom Training Unit, No 767 Squadron, was formed in January 1969 in preparation for what was to be the sole operational squadron, No 892, which had previously been equipped with the Sea Vixen FAW.2.

Carrier training was provided to 892's pilots aboard the USS *Saratoga* in the autumn of 1969 before the unit's first embarkation in HMS *Ark Royal,* in June 1970.

Ark Royal was finally paid off in 1978 and surviving Royal Navy Phantoms were transferred to the RAF to augment Air Force air-defence squadrons.

Phantom FG.1 of 892 Squadron during cross-operations on board USS *Saratoga*

Phantom FG.1 approaching the round-down

Westland Sea King

The Sea King was developed to meet a Royal Navy requirement for a sophisticated anti-submarine helicopter capable of maintaining extended patrols under the worst weather conditions. No less important are its secondary roles of search and rescue, casualty evacuation and troop transport, although the latter role is generally performed by the Navy's version of the Westland Commando, the Sea King HC.4.

British Sea King development stemmed from a licence agreement with Sikorsky covering the S-61 helicopter, concluded in 1959. Using the basic airframe of the US SH-3D, Westland fitted two Rolls-Royce Gnome turboshafts, AW391 radar in a dorsal radome aft of the engine casing, Plessey 195 dipping sonar and an advanced flight-control system. In addition, the Royal Navy version was to have power-folding main

rotor blades and a retractable undercarriage housed in twin sponsons.

The first version was the Sea King HAS.1, ordered in 1967. The first production example, XV642, flew for the first time on May 7, 1969. After passing through the Intensive Flying Trials Unit, No 700S Flight, which commissioned at RNAS Culdrose in August 1969, the Mk 1 was issued to Nos 814, 819, 820, 824 and 826 Squadrons. First of these units to be equipped was 824 Squadron, which formed at Culdrose in February 1970, subsequently embarking in HMS *Ark Royal*. A total of 56 had been built when production ended in May 1972. Surviving aircraft are currently being uprated to Mk 2 standard.

The Sea King HAS.2 incorporates a number of improvements to both the airframe and the equipment. It

was first flown on June 18, 1976, and a total of 21 were ordered. First operational unit to re-equip was No 826 Squadron, at Culdrose in December 1976. The Mk 2s are in turn being uprated to Mk 5 standard by the introduction of the Marconi Avionics LAPADS (Lightweight Acoustic Processing and Display System) passive sonobuoy processor and other avionics improvements. The Royal Navy ordered 17 of the new variant and the first pair were handed over in October 1980.

For troop-carrying the Navy ordered 15 Sea King HC.4s, a version of the land-based Commando. It features the folding rotor blades and folding tail pylon of the ASW Sea King but incorporates the fixed landing gear of the Commando. First flown on September 26, 1979, the type currently equips Nos 845 and 846 (Naval Air Commando) Squadrons.

Sea King HAS.1s from 700S Squadron, Culdrose

Sea King HC.4 utility helicopter

Prototype Sea King HAS.5, converted from a Mk 2

Westland/Aérospatiale Gazelle

The Gazelle is one of a number of helicopters covered by the Anglo-French agreement signed in 1967. Several versions are produced for different operators, and that selected for the Royal Navy is the SA.341C Gazelle HT.2.

The first prototype, designated SA.340, flew for the first time on April 7, 1967, followed by a second aircraft a year later. The first production Gazelle flew in August 1971.

The Royal Navy ordered 30 Gazelle HT.2s to replace its Hillers and Whirlwinds in the training role. First production Navy aircraft, XW845, made its first flight in 1973 and the type entered service at RNAS Culdrose in December 1977. From the following March, when the final Hiller departed, the Gazelle formed the sole equipment of 705 Squadron.

Six Culdrose-based Gazelles from 705 Squadron

Westland Lynx

The Lynx is one of three helicopters covered by the 1967 Anglo-French helicopter agreement, the other two being the Puma and the Gazelle. The Royal Navy's Lynx HAS.2 was designed to supersede the Wasp HAS.1 as the Royal Navy's standard Small Ships Flight anti-submarine hunter-killer and is widely deployed aboard Royal Navy frigates and destroyers.

The first Navy Lynx flew for the first time on May 20, 1972, and the type entered service with the Fleet Air Arm in September 1976 when the Intensive Flying Trials Unit, No 700L Squadron, was formed to train Royal Navy and Dutch pilots. Deck-handling tests aboard HMS *Birmingham* were completed in February 1977. Following the completion of

intensive trials in December 1977, No 700L Squadron was reformed as 702 Headquarters Squadron. This in turn was relegated to a training role when 815 Squadron was formed at Yeovilton on January 29, 1981, to take over as headquarters squadron. Total production is scheduled to reach 80 aircraft.

The Naval Lynx can carry a formidable array of

anti-submarine weapons, including two Mk 44 or Mk 46 homing torpedoes and six marine markers, or two Mk 11 nuclear depth charges. For attacking surface shipping the Lynx carries four Sea Skua semi-active homing missiles or four AS.12 wire-guided missiles.

British Aerospace Sea Harrier

At a time when it seemed certain that the Fleet Air Arm was to lose for all time its fixed-wing element, the British Government announced that it was to proceed with the development of a maritime version of the V/Stol Harrier, to be designated Sea Harrier FRS.1.

The decision to go ahead with the Sea Harrier, announced in May 1975, had a lot to do with the laying down in 1973 of the first of a new type of aircraft carrier, the "through-deck cruiser" HMS *Invincible*. Though she was originally

planned as a helicopter carrier, it was soon realised that she could operate V/Stol aircraft with relatively little change to her basic design. One vital subsequent change to the *Invincible* class was the provision of a "ski-jump" ramp at the forward end of the flight deck to enable the aircraft to take off more heavily loaded than would otherwise be possible.

The first Sea Harrier to fly made its first flight on August 20, 1978, and the first production aircraft was handed over in the following June. Deck-handling trials were carried out from HMS

Hermes during November 1979, following the commissioning of the Intensive Flying Trials Unit, No 700A Squadron, at RNAS Yeovilton on September 19. On March 31, 1980, No 700A Squadron became No 899 Headquarters Squadron and at the same time the first operational squadron, No 800, was formed.

With an initial planned buy of 34 FRS.1s and up to four two-seat T.4s, the policy was to have one headquarters squadron (No 899) of seven aircraft and two operational squadrons (Nos 800 and 801) of

five aircraft each, the balance forming attrition reserves until 1990. The second operational squadron, 801, formed at Yeovilton on February 26, 1981.

Major changes compared with the RAF Harrier GR.3 include a new raised cockpit reminiscent of that of the Sea Hawk, revised avionics and the installation of the multi-mode Blue Fox radar housed in a redesigned nose. To stave off the ravages of sea-water corrosion, most of the magnesium components have been replaced by aluminium alloy units.

Sea Harrier FRS.1 XZ454 from 800 Squadron

Sea Harrier FRS.1s of No 899 Squadron (front), No 800 Squadron (middle) and No 801 Squadron (rear)

Data

Type	Powerplant	Dimensions	Weights	Performance	Armament	Crew
Short Type 184	1×225/240/260 hp Sunbeam; 240 hp Renault or 275 hp Sunbeam Maori III	Span: 63ft 6¼in Length: 40ft 7½in Height: 13ft 6in Wing area: 688 sq ft	Empty: 3,703lb Gross: 5,363lb	Max speed: 88½ mph at 2,000ft Ceiling: 9,000ft Endurance: 2¾hr	1×0.303in Lewis; 1×14in torpedo or 520lb bombs	2
Avro 504	1×80 hp Gnome	Span: 36ft Length: 29ft 5in Height: 10ft 5in Wing area: 330 sq ft	Empty: 924lb Gross: 1,574lb	Max speed: 82 mph at S/L Endurance: 4½hr	up to 80lb bombs	1
Curtiss JN-4	1×90 hp Curtiss OX-5	Span: 43ft 9in Length: 27ft 4in Height: 9ft 10½in Wing area: 352 sq ft	Empty: 1,580lb Gross: 2,130lb	Max speed: 75 mph Ceiling: 8,000ft Range: 250 miles	—	2
Sopwith Tabloid	1×100 hp Gnome Monosoupape	Span: 25ft 6in Length: 20ft 4in Height: 8ft 5in Wing area: 241 sq ft	Empty: 730lb Gross: 1,120lb	Max speed: 92mph at S/L Endurance: 3½hr	1×0.303in Lewis	1
Caudron G.IV	2×80 hp Le Rhône or 2×100 hp Anzani	Span: 55ft 5in Length: 23ft 6in Height: 8ft 5in Wing area: 427½ sq ft	Empty: 1,870lb Gross: 2,970lb	Max speed: 82 mph at 6,500ft Ceiling: 14,000ft Endurance: 4hr	1×0.303in mg	2
Sopwith Schneider	1×100 hp Gnome Monosoupape	Span: 25ft 8in Length: 22ft 10in Height: 10ft Wing area: 240 sq ft	Empty: 1,220lb Gross: 1,700lb	Max speed: 87 mph Ceiling: 8,000ft	1×Lewis mg; 1×65lb bomb	1
Curtiss H.4 Small America	2×90 hp Curtiss OX-5 or 100 hp Anzani or 110 hp Clerget	Span: 72ft 0in Length: 36ft 0in Height: 16ft 0in Wing area: —	Empty: 2,992lb Gross: 4,983lb	No details available	1×mg; bombs	4
BE.2C	1×70 hp Renault; 90 hp RAF.1A or 90 hp Curtiss OX-5	Span: 37ft Length: 27ft 3in Height: 11ft 1½in Wing area: 371 sq ft	Empty: 1,370lb Gross: 2,142lb	Max speed: 72 mph at 6,500ft Ceiling: 10,000ft Endurance: 3¼hr	up to 4×25lb bombs (Renault) or 2×112lb bombs (RAF)	2
Bristol Scout C	1×80 hp Gnome	Span: 24ft 7in Length: 20ft 8in Height: 8ft 6in Wing area: 198 sq ft	Empty: 750lb Gross: 1,190lb	Max speed: 93 mph at S/L Ceiling: 15,000ft Endurance: 2½hr	48 Ranken darts or 1×Lewis mg (Scout D)	1
Henri Farman	1×80 hp Gnome	Span: 44ft 9in Length: 26ft 6in Height: 12ft Wing area: 375 sq ft	Empty: 820lb Gross: 1,440lb	Max speed: 60 mph at S/L Endurance: 3hr	—	2
Nieuport Scout	1×110 hp Le Rhône	Span: 27ft 3in Length: 19ft 6in Height: 7ft Wing area: 158 sq ft	Empty: 825lb Gross: 1,233lb	Max speed: 107 mph at 6,500ft Ceiling: 17,400ft Endurance: 2hr	1×Lewis mg; (later also 1× synchronised Vickers)	1
Short Bomber	1×225 hp Sunbeam or 250 hp Rolls-Royce Eagle	Span: 85ft Length: 45ft Height: 15ft Wing area: 870 sq ft	Gross: 6,800lb	Max speed: 77 mph at 6,500ft Ceiling: 9,500ft Endurance: 6hr	1×Lewis mg; 4×230lb bombs or 8×112lb bombs	2
Sopwith Baby	1×110 or 130 hp Clerget	Span: 25ft 8in Length: 23ft Height: 10ft Wing area: 240 sq ft	Empty: 1,226lb Gross: 1,715lb	Max speed: 100 mph at S/L Endurance: 2¼hr	1×Lewis mg; 2×65lb bombs	1

Type	Powerplant	Dimensions	Weights	Performance	Armament	Crew
Short 827	1×150 hp Sunbeam Nubian	Span: 53ft 11in Length: 35ft 3in Height: 13ft 6in Wing area: 506 sq ft	Gross: 3,400lb	Max speed: 61 mph	1×Lewis mg; bombs	2
Nieuport Two-Seater	1×110 hp or 130 hp Clerget	Span: 29ft 7½in Length: 23ft 11¼in Height: 8ft 9in Wing area: 236½ sq ft	Empty: 1,210lb Gross: 2,026lb	Max speed: 78 mph at 5,000ft Ceiling: 13,000ft Endurance: 3hr	1×Lewis mg	1
Wight Converted Seaplane	1×322 hp Rolls-Royce Eagle VI or 265 hp Sunbeam Maori	Span: 65 ft 6in Length: 44ft 8½in Height: 16ft Wing area: 715 sq ft	Empty: 3,758lb Gross: 5,556lb	Max speed: 84 mph at 2,000ft Ceiling: 9,600ft Endurance: 3½hr	1×Lewis mg; 4×100lb or 112lb bombs	2
Norman Thompson NT.4	2×200 hp Hispano-Suiza	Span: 78ft 7in Length: 41ft 6in Height: 14ft 10in Wing area: 936 sq ft	Empty: 4,572lb Gross: 6,469lb	Max speed: 95 mph at 2,000ft Ceiling: 11,700ft	1×Lewis mg; bombs	4
Sopwith 1½-Strutter	1×110 hp or 130 hp Clerget	Span: 33ft 6in Length: 25ft 3in Height: 10ft 3in Wing area: 346 sq ft	Empty: 1,259lb Gross: 2,149lb	Max speed: 106 mph at S/L Ceiling: 13,000ft Endurance: 4½hr	2-seater: 1×Vickers mg; 2×65lb bombs	2
Morane-Saulnier Type L	1×80 hp Le Rhône	Span: 34ft Length: 20ft 9in Height: 11ft 5in Wing area: 172 sq ft	Gross: 839lb	Max speed: 76 mph	—	2
Pemberton-Billing PB.25	1×110 hp Clerget or 100 hp Gnome Monosoupape	Span: 32ft 11½in Length: 24ft 1in Height: 10ft 5in Wing area: 277 sq ft	Empty: 1,108lb Gross: 1,541lb	Max speed: 89 mph at S/L Endurance: 2½hr	1×Lewis mg	1
de Havilland DH.6	1×90 hp RAF.1A; 90 hp Curtiss OX-5 or 80 hp Renault	Span: 35ft 11in Length: 27ft 3½in Height: 20ft 9½in Wing area: 436 sq ft	Empty: 1,460lb Gross: 2,027lb	Max speed: 75 mph at 2,000ft Ceiling: 6,100ft	up to 100lb bombs	2
Sopwith Pup	1×80 hp Le Rhône	Span: 26ft 6in Length: 19ft 3¼in Height: 9ft 5in Wing area: 254 sq ft	Empty: 787lb Gross: 1,225lb	Max speed: 111½ mph at S/L Ceiling: 17,500ft Endurance: 3hr	1×Vickers mg (shore-based); 1×Lewis or 8×Le Prieur rockets (shipborne)	1
Sopwith Triplane	1×110 hp or 130 hp Clerget	Span: 26ft 6in Length: 18ft 10in Height: 10ft 6in Wing area: 231 sq ft	Empty: 1,101lb Gross: 1,541lb	Max speed: 117 mph at 5,000ft Ceiling: 20,500ft Endurance: 2¾hr	1×Vickers mg	1
Handley Page O/100	2×266 hp Rolls-Royce Eagle II or 2×320 hp Sunbeam Cossack	Span: 100ft Length: 62ft 10¼in Height: 22ft Wing area: 1,648 sq ft	Empty: 8,000lb Gross: 14,000lb	Max speed: 85 mph	up to 5×Lewis mg; 16×112lb bombs	4
Short 320 seaplane	1×310 hp or 320 hp Sunbeam Cossack	Span: 75ft Length: 45ft 9in Height: 17ft 6in Wing area: 810 sq ft	Empty: 4,933lb Gross: 7,014lb	Max speed: 72½ mph at 1,200ft Ceiling: 3,000ft	1×Lewis mg; 1×18in torpedo or 2×230lb bombs	2
AD Flying Boat	1×200 hp Hispano-Suiza	Span: 50ft 0in Length: 30ft 3in Height: 12ft 3in Wing area: 487 sq ft	Empty: 2,467lb Gross: 3,561lb	Max speed: 98½ mph at 1,000ft Ceiling: 14,400ft Endurance: 4½hr	—	2
Sopwith F.1 Camel	1×130 hp Clerget or 150 hp Bentley BR.1	Span: 28ft Length: 18ft 9in Height: 8ft 6in Wing area: 231 sq ft	Empty: 929lb Gross: 1,453lb	Max speed: 115 mph at 6,500ft Ceiling: 19,000ft Endurance: 2½hr	2×Vickers mg; up to 100lb bombs	1
Sopwith 2F.1 Camel	1×130 hp Clerget or 150 hp Bentley BR.1	Span: 26ft 11in Length: 18ft 8in Height: 9ft 1in Wing area: 221 sq ft	Empty: 1,036lb Gross: 1,530lb	Max speed: 124 mph at 6,500ft Ceiling: 17,300ft	1×Vickers mg; 1×Lewis mg; 100lb bombs	2

Type	Powerplant	Dimensions	Weights	Performance	Armament	Crew
Fairey Hamble Baby	1×110 hp or 130 hp Clerget	Span: 27ft 9¼in Length: 23ft 4in Height: 9ft 6in Wing area: 246 sq ft	Empty: 1,386lb Gross: 1,946lb	Max speed: 90 mph at 2,000ft Service ceiling: 7,600ft Endurance: 2hr	1×Lewis mg; 2×65lb bombs	1
Curtiss H.12 Large America	2×345 hp Rolls-Royce Eagle VII or 375 hp Eagle VIII	Span: 92ft 8½in Length: 46ft 6in Height: 16ft 6in Wing area: 1,216 sq ft	Empty: 7,293lb Gross: 10,650lb	Max speed: 85 mph at 2,000ft Ceiling: 10,800ft Endurance: 6hr	4×Lewis mg; up to 500lb bombs	4
Sopwith Cuckoo	1×200 hp Sunbeam Arab	Span: 46ft 9in Length: 28ft 6in Height: 10ft 8in Wing area: 566 sq ft	Empty: 2,199lb Gross: 3,883lb	Max speed: 103½ mph at 2,000ft Service ceiling: 12,100ft Endurance: 4hr	1×18in Mk IX torpedo	1
Felixstowe F.2A	2×345 hp Rolls-Royce Eagle VIII	Span: 95ft 7½in Length: 46ft 3in Height: 17ft 6in	Empty: 7,549lb Gross: 10,978lb	Max speed: 95½ mph at 2,000ft Service ceiling: 9,600ft Endurance: 6hr	4/7 Lewis mg; 2×230lb bombs	4
Fairey Campania	1×275 hp Sunbeam Maori II or 345 hp Rolls-Royce Eagle VIII	Span: 61ft 7½in Length: 43ft 0½in Height: 15ft 1in Wing area: 627 sq ft	Empty: 3,874lb Gross: 5,657lb	Max speed: 80 mph at 2,000ft Service ceiling: 5,500ft Endurance: 3hr	1×Lewis mg; bombs	2
Beardmore WB.III	1×80 hp Le Rhône or 80 hp Clerget	Span: 25ft 0in Length: 20ft 2½in Height: 8ft 1¼in Wing area: 243 sq ft	Empty: 890lb Gross: 1,289lb	Max speed: 103 mph at S/L Service ceiling: 12,400ft Endurance: 2¾hr	1×Lewis mg	1
Fairey IIIC	1×375 hp Rolls-Royce Eagle VIII	Span: 46ft 1¼in Length: 36ft 0in Height: 12ft 1¾in Wing area: 542 sq ft	Empty: 3,392lb Gross: 4,800lb	Max speed: 110½ mph at 10,000ft Service ceiling: 15,000ft Endurance: 5½hr	1×Vickers mg; 1×Lewis mg; bombs	2
Curtiss H.16 Large America	2×345 hp Rolls-Royce Eagle VIII	Span: 95ft Length: 46ft 1½in Height: 17ft 8in Wing area: 1,200 sq ft	Empty: 7,363lb Gross: 10,670lb	Max speed: 98 mph at 2,000ft Ceiling: 12,500ft Endurance: 6hr	1×twin Lewis mg; bombs	4
de Havilland DH.9	1×230 hp BHP or Siddeley Puma	Span: 42ft 4½in Length: 30ft 6in Height: 11ft 2in Wing area: 434 sq ft	Empty: 2,203lb Gross: 3,669lb	Max speed: 111½ mph at 10,000ft Service ceiling: 15,500ft Endurance: 4½hr	1×Vickers mg; 1×Lewis mg; 2×230lb or 4×112lb bombs	2
Parnall Panther	1×230 hp Bentley BR.2	Span: 29ft 6in Length: 24ft 11in Height: 10ft 6in Wing area: 336 sq ft	Empty: 1,328lb Gross: 2,595lb	Max speed: 108½ mph at 6,500ft Service ceiling: 14,500ft Endurance: 4½hr	1×Lewis mg	2
Westland Walrus	1×450 hp Napier Lion II	Span: 45ft 10in Length: 30ft 0in Height: 11ft 7in Wing area: 496 sq ft	Gross: 4,994lb	Max speed: 124 mph	1×Vickers mg	3
Nieuport Nightjar	1×230 hp Bentley BR.2	Span: 28ft 0in Length: 19ft 2in Height: 9ft 7in Wing area: 270 sq ft	Gross: 2,165lb	Max speed: 120 mph at S/L Service ceiling: 15,000ft Endurance: 2hr	2×Vickers mg	1
Avro Bison	1×480 hp Napier Lion II	Span: 46ft 0in Length: 36ft 0in Height: 14ft 2in Wing area: 630 sq ft	Empty: 4,116lb Gross: 6,132lb	Max speed: 110 mph Cruising speed: 90 mph Service ceiling: 12,000ft Range: 360 miles	1×Lewis mg; 1×Vickers mg	3/4
Parnall Plover	1×436 hp Bristol Jupiter IV	Span: 29ft 0in Length: 23ft 0in Height: 12ft 0in Wing area: 306 sq ft	Empty: 2,035lb Gross: 2,984lb	Max speed: 142 mph Service ceiling: 23,000ft	2×Vickers mg	1
Fairey Flycatcher	1×400 hp Armstrong Siddeley Jaguar III/IV	Span: 29ft 0in Length: 23ft 0in Height: 12ft 0in Wing area: 288 sq ft	Empty: 2,039lb Gross: 3,028lb	Max speed: 133 mph at 5,000ft Service ceiling: 19,000ft Range: 263 miles at 10,000ft	2×Vickers mg; 4×20lb bombs	1

Type	Powerplant	Dimensions	Weights	Performance	Armament	Crew
Blackburn Dart	1×450 hp Napier Lion IIB/V	Span: 45ft 6in Length: 35ft 4½in Height: 12ft 11in Wing area: 654 sq ft	Empty: 3,599lb Gross: 6,383lb	Max speed: 107 mph at 3,000ft Service ceiling: 12,700ft Range: 285 miles	1×18in torpedo	1
Supermarine Seagull III	1×450 hp Napier Lion V	Span: 46ft 0in Length: 37ft 0in Height: 12ft 0in Wing area: 593 sq ft	Empty: 3,897lb Gross: 5,668lb	Max speed: 108 mph at S/L	1×Lewis mg	3
Fairey IIID	1×375 hp Rolls-Royce Eagle VIII or 450 hp Napier Lion	Span: 46ft 2¼in length: 37ft 0in Height: 11ft 4in Wing area: 500 sq ft	Empty: 3,990lb Gross: 5,050lb	Max speed: 106 mph Service ceiling: 16,500ft Range: 550 miles at 100 mph	1×Vickers mg; 1×Lewis mg	3
Blackburn Blackburn	1×450 hp Napier Lion IIB/V	Span: 45ft 6½in Length: 36ft 2in Height: 12ft 6in Wing area: 650 sq ft	Empty: 3,929lb Gross: 5,962lb	Max speed: 122 mph at 3,000ft Service ceiling: 12,950ft Range: 440 miles	1×Lewis mg; 1×Vickers mg	3/4
Fairey IIIF	1×570 hp Napier Lion XIA	Span: 45ft 9½in Length: 34ft 4in Height: 14ft 2¾in Wing area: 443½ sq ft	Empty: 3,923lb Gross: 6,301lb	Max speed: 120 mph at 10,000ft Service ceiling: 20,000ft Endurance: 3/4hr	1×Vickers mg; 1×Lewis mg; up to 500lb bombs	3
Parnall Peto	1×135 hp Armstrong Siddeley Mongoose	Span: 28ft 5in Length: 22ft 6¼in	Gross: 1,950lb	Max speed: 113 mph at S/L Endurance: 2hr	—	2
Blackburn Ripon	1×570 hp Napier Lion XIA	Span: 44ft 10in Length: 36ft 9in Height: 13ft 4in Wing area: 683 sq ft	Empty: 4,255lb Gross: 7,405lb	Max speed: 126 mph at S/L Cruising: 109 mph Service ceiling: 10,000ft Range: 815 miles with torpedo	1×Vickers mg; 1×Lewis mg; 1×Mk VIII or X torpedo	2
Hawker Nimrod	1×590 hp Rolls-Royce Kestrel IIS	Span: 33ft 6¼in Length: 26ft 11¾in Height: 9ft 9in Wing area: 298½ sq ft	Empty: 3,065lb Gross: 4,258lb	Max speed: 195 mph at 14,000ft Service ceiling: 26,000ft Endurance: 1.65hr at 10,000ft	2×Vickers mg	1
Hawker Osprey	1×640hp Rolls-Royce Kestrel V	Span: 37ft 0in Length: 29ft 4in Height: 10ft 5in Wing area: 339 sq ft	Empty: 3,405lb Gross: 4,950lb	Max speed: 168 mph at 5,000ft Service ceiling: 23,500ft	1×Vickers mg; 1×Lewis mg; 2×112lb bombs	2
Fairey Seal	1×525 hp Armstrong Siddeley Panther IIA	Span: 45ft 9in Length: 33ft 8in Height: 12ft 9in Wing area: 443½ sq ft	Gross: 6,000lb	Max speed: 138 mph Service ceiling: 17,000ft Endurance: 4½hr	1×Vickers mg; 1×Lewis mg; up to 500lb bombs	3
Supermarine Walrus	1×775hp Bristol Pegasus	Span: 45ft 10in Length: 37ft 3in Height: 15ft 3in Wing area: 610 sq ft	Empty: 4,900lb Gross: 7,200lb	Max speed: 135 mph at 4,750ft Cruising: 95 mph Service ceiling: 18,500ft Range: 600 miles	2/3 Vickers K mg	3
Blackburn Baffin	1×565 hp Bristol Pegasus IM.3	Span: 45ft 6½in Length: 38ft 3¾in Height: 13ft 5½in Wing area: 683 sq ft	Empty: 3,184lb Gross: 7,610lb	Max speed: 136 mph at 6,500ft Service ceiling: 15,000ft Range: 450 miles at 100 mph	1×Vickers mg; 1×Lewis mg; 1×Mk VIII or X torpedo or up to 2,000lb bombs	2
Blackburn Shark	1×760 hp Armstrong Siddeley Tiger VI	Span: 46ft 0in Length: 35ft 2¼in Height: 12ft 1in Wing area: 489 sq ft	Empty: 4,039lb Gross: 8,050lb	Max speed: 152 mph at 6,500ft Cruising: 118 mph Service ceiling: 16,400ft Range: 1,130 miles	1×Vickers mg; 1×Lewis mg; 1×1,500lb torpedo or bombs	2/3
Fairey Swordfish	1×690 hp Bristol Pegasus IIIM or 750 hp Pegasus XXX	Span: 45ft 6in Length: 36ft 4in Height: 12ft 10in Wing area: 607 sq ft	Empty: 5,200lb Gross: 9,250lb	Max speed: 139 mph at 4,750ft Cruising: 104 mph at 5,000ft Service ceiling: 10,700ft Tactical range: 546 miles	1×Vickers mg; 1×Lewis mg; 1×18in torpedo or up to 1,500lb bombs	2/3

Type	Powerplant	Dimensions	Weights	Performance	Armament	Crew
Fairey Seafox	1×395 hp Napier Rapier VI	Span: 40ft 0in Length: 35ft 5½in Height: 12ft 1in Wing area: 434 sq ft	Empty: 3,805lb Gross: 5,420lb	Max speed: 124 mph at 5,860ft Cruising: 106 mph Service ceiling: 9,700ft Range: 440 miles	1×Lewis mg	2
Blackburn Skua	1×890 hp Bristol Perseus XII	Span: 46ft 2in Length: 35ft 7in Height: 12ft 6in Wing area: 319 sq ft	Empty: 5,490lb Gross: 8,228lb	Max speed: 225 mph at 6,500ft Cruising: 144/165 mph at 15,000ft Service ceiling: 19,100ft Range: 760 miles	4×Browning mg; 1×Lewis mg; 1×500lb bomb	2
Gloster Sea Gladiator	1×840 hp Bristol Mercury VIIIA	Span: 32ft 3in Length: 27ft 5in Height: 10ft 4in Wing area: 323 sq ft	Empty: 3,553lb Gross: 5,019lb	Max speed: 245 mph at 10,000ft Cruising: 212 mph at 15,000ft Service ceiling: 32,000ft Range: 425 miles	4×Browning mg	1
de Havilland Dominie	2×200 hp DH Gipsy Six	Span: 48ft 0in Length: 34ft 6in Height: 10ft 3in Wing area: 336 sq ft	Empty: 3,346lb Gross: 5,500lb	Max speed: 157 mph Cruising: 132 mph Ceiling: 19,500ft Range: 578 miles	—	10
Grumman Martlet	1×1,200 hp Wright Cyclone G-205A	Span: 38ft 0in Length: 28ft 10in Height: 9ft 2½in Wing area: 260 sq ft	Empty: 4,425lb Gross: 5,876lb	Max speed: 310 mph Cruising: 257 mph Ceiling: 28,000ft Range: 1,100 miles	4×0.50-cal mg	1
Grumman Wildcat IV	1×1,200 hp Pratt & Whitney Twin Wasp R-1830-86	Span: 38ft 0in Length: 28ft 11in Height: 9ft 2½in Wing area: 260 sq ft	Empty: 4,649lb Gross: 6,100lb	Max speed: 330 mph at 19,500ft Cruising: 297 mph at 19,500ft Ceiling: 28,000ft Max range: 1,150 miles	6×0.50-cal mg	1
Blackburn Roc	1×890 hp Bristol Perseus XII	Span: 46ft 0in Length: 35ft 7in Height: 12ft 1in Wing area: 310 sq ft	Empty: 6,121lb Gross: 7,950lb	Max speed: 223 mph at 10,000ft Cruising: 135 mph Ceiling: 18,000ft Range: 810 miles	4×Browning mg in turret	2
Fairey Albacore	1×1,065 hp Bristol Taurus II or 1,130 hp Taurus XII	Span: 50ft 0in Length: 39ft 9½in Height: 15 ft 3in Wing area: 623 sq ft	Empty: 7,200lb Gross: 12,600lb	Max speed: 161 mph at 6,000ft Cruising: 116 mph at 6,000ft Ceiling: 20,700ft Range: 930 miles with 1,610lb load	3×Vickers mg; 1×18in torpedo or 2,000lb bombs	3
Fairey Fulmar	1×1,080 hp Rolls-Royce Merlin VIII	Span: 46ft 4½in Length: 40ft 3in Height: 14ft 0in Wing area: 342 sq ft	Empty: 6,915lb Gross: 9,800lb	Max speed: 256 mph at 2,400ft Ceiling: 22,400ft Range: 830 miles	8×Browning mg; 2×250lb bombs	2
Curtiss Seamew	1×520 hp Ranger SGV-770-6	Span: 38ft 0in Length: 36ft 10in Height: 11ft 5in Wing area: 290 sq ft	Empty: 4,284lb Gross: 5,729lb	Max speed: 190 mph at 7,500ft Cruising: 126 mph Endurance: 8hr	2×mg	2
Hawker Sea Hurricane	1×1,460 hp Rolls-Royce Merlin XX	Span: 40ft 0in Length: 32ft 3in Height: 13 ft 3in Wing area: 258 sq ft	Empty: 5,800lb Gross: 7,800lb	Max speed: 342 mph at 22,000ft Cruising: 212/292 mph at 20,000ft Ceiling: 35,600ft Range: 460 miles	4×20 mm cannon	1
Supermarine Seafire IB	1×1,340 hp Rolls-Royce Merlin 45/46	Span: 36ft 8in Length: 30ft 0in Height: 11ft 2in Wing area: 242 sq ft	Empty: 5,000lb Gross: 6,700lb	Max speed: 365 mph at 16,000ft Cruising: 215 mph at 20,000ft Ceiling: 36,400ft Range: 492 miles	2×20mm cannon; 4×mg	1

Type	Powerplant	Dimensions	Weights	Performance	Armament	Crew
Vought-Sikorsky Chesapeake	1×750 hp Pratt & Whitney Twin Wasp Junior SB4-G	Span: 42ft 0in Length: 33ft 11¾in Height: 9ft 9½in Wing area: 305 sq ft	Empty: 4,500lb Gross: 6,500lb	Max speed: 257 mph at 11,000ft Cruising: 210 mph Ceiling: 28,200ft Range: 700 miles	5×mg; 3×500lb bombs	2
Vought-Sikorsky Kingfisher	1×450 hp Pratt & Whitney Wasp Junior R-985-SB3	Span: 35ft 11in Length: 33ft 7¾in Height: 14ft 8in	Empty: 3,335lb Gross: 4,980lb	Max speed: 171 mph Cruising: 152 mph Ceiling: 18,200ft Range: 908 miles	2×mg; up to 240lb bombs	2
Fairey Barracuda I	1×1,260 hp Rolls-Royce Merlin 30	Span: 49ft 2in Length: 39ft 9in Height: 15ft 1in Wing area: 367 sq ft	Empty: 8,700lb Gross: 13,500lb	Max speed: 235 mph at 11,000ft Cruising: 138 mph at 6,000ft Ceiling: 18,400ft Range: 524 miles with 2,000lb load	2×Vickers K mg; 1×1,610lb torpedo or up to 2,000lb bombs	3
Fairey Barracuda V	1×2,020 hp Rolls-Royce Griffon 37	Span: 53ft 0½in Length: 41ft 1in Height: 13ft 2½in Wing area: 435 sq ft	Empty: 11,430lb Gross: 16,000lb	Max speed: 253 mph at 10,000ft Ceiling: 24,000ft Range: 600 miles with 2,000lb load	2,000lb external bombs	2
Grumman Avenger TR.I	1×1,850 hp Wright Cyclone GR-2600-8	Span: 54ft 2in Length: 40ft 0in Height: 15ft 8in Wing area: 490 sq ft	Empty: 10,600lb Gross: 16,300lb	Max speed: 259 mph at 11,200ft Cruising: 171 mph at 5,000ft Ceiling: 23,000ft Range: 1,020 miles	2×fixed 0.50-cal mg; 1×0.30-cal mg; 1×0.50-cal mg; 1×22in torpedo or up to 2,000lb bombs	3
Grumman Avenger AS.4	1×1,750 hp Wright Cyclone R-2600-20	Span: 54ft 2in Length: 40ft 0in Height: 15ft 8in Wing area: 490 sq ft	Empty: 10,700lb Gross: 16,671lb	Max speed: 261 mph Cruising: 151 mph Ceiling: 22,600ft Range: 1,130 miles	up to 2,000lb bombs or depth charges; 8×60lb RP	3
Chance-Vought Corsair I	1×2,000 hp Pratt & Whitney Twin Wasp R-2800-8	Span: 41ft 0in Length: 33ft 4in Height: 15ft 1in Wing area: 314 sq ft	Empty: 8,800lb Gross: 11,800lb	Max speed: 374 mph at 23,000ft Cruising: 251 mph at 20,000ft Ceiling: 34,500ft Range: 673 miles	4×0.50-cal mg	1
Blackburn Firebrand TF.5	1×2,520 hp Bristol Centaurus IX	Span: 51ft 3½in Length: 38ft 9in Height: 13ft 3in Wing area: 383 sq ft	Empty: 11,835lb Gross: 17,500lb	Max speed: 340 mph at 13,000ft Cruising: 256 mph Ceiling: 31,000ft Range: 740 miles at 256 mph	4×Hispano cannon; up to 2,000lb bombs or torpedo	1
Grumman Hellcat II	1×2,000 hp Pratt & Whitney Double Wasp R-2800-10W	Span: 42ft 10in Length: 33ft 7in Height: 14ft 5in Wing area: 334 sq ft	Empty: 9,212lb Gross: 12,727lb	Max speed: 371 mph at 17,200ft Cruising: 159 mph Ceiling: 36,700ft Range: 1,040 miles at 159 mph	6×0.50-cal mg; 6×60lb RP or 2×1,000lb bombs	1
Fairey Firefly F.1	1×1,730 hp Rolls-Royce Griffon IIB or 1,990 hp Griffon XII	Span: 44ft 6in Length: 37ft 7¼in Height: 13ft 7in Wing area: 328 sq ft	Empty: 9,750lb Gross: 14,020lb	Max speed: 316 mph at 14,000ft Ceiling: 28,000ft Range: 1,300 miles	4×20mm cannon; 8×60lb RP or 2×1,000lb bombs	2
Fairey Firefly AS.5	1×2,250 hp Rolls-Royce Griffon 74	Span: 41 ft 2in Length: 27ft 11in Height: 14ft 4in Wing area: 330 sq ft	Empty: 9,674lb Gross: 16,096lb	Max speed: 386 mph at 14,000ft Cruising: 220 mph Ceiling: 28,400ft Range: 660 miles	4×20 mm cannon; 16×60lb RP or 2×1,000lb bombs	2
Supermarine Seafire 47	1×2,375 hp Rolls-Royce Griffon 85	Span: 36ft 11in Length: 34ft 4in Height: 12ft 9in Wing area: 244 sq ft	Empty: 7,625lb Gross: 11,615lb	Max speed: 452 mph at 20,500ft Ceiling: 43,100ft Range: 400 miles	4×20 mm cannon; 8×60lb RP or 3×500lb bombs	1

Type	Powerplant	Dimensions	Weights	Performance	Armament	Crew
Supermarine Sea Otter	1×855 hp Bristol Mercury XXX	Span: 46ft 0in Length: 39ft 5in Height: 16ft 2in Wing area: 610 sq ft	Empty: 6,805lb Gross: 10,000lb	Max speed: 150 mph at 5,000ft Cruising: 100 mph Ceiling: 16,000ft Range: 725 miles	3×Vickers K mg	3/4
Miles Monitor	2×1,750 hp Wright R-2600-31 Double-Row Cyclone	Span: 55ft 3in Length: 46ft 8in Height: 13ft 9in Wing area: 500 sq ft	Empty: 15,723lb Gross: 21,056lb	Max speed: 360 mph at 20,000ft Cruising: 300 mph at 20,000ft Range: 1,000 miles	—	2
de Havilland Sea Mosquito TR.33	2×1,640 hp Rolls-Royce Merlin 25	Span: 54ft 2in Length: 42ft 3in Height: 13ft 6in Wing area: 454 sq ft	Empty: 17,165lb Gross: 22,500lb	Max speed: 385 mph at 13,500ft Ceiling: 30,000ft Range: 1,260 miles	4×Hispano 20mm cannon; 8×60lb RP or 1×18in torpedo or 2,000lb bombs	2
Sikorsky Hoverfly I	1×180 hp Warner R-550	Rotor dia: 38ft Length: 35ft 3in Height: 12ft 5in	Empty: 2,020lb Gross: 2,535lb	Max speed: 75 mph at S/L Ceiling: 8,000ft Range: 130 miles	—	2
Sikorsky Hoverfly II	1×240 hp Franklin O-405-9	Rotor dia: 38ft 0in Length: 38ft 3in	Gross: 2,590lb	Max speed: 96 mph at S/L	—	2
Supermarine Seafang 32	1×2,375 hp Rolls-Royce Griffon 89	Span: 35ft 0in Length: 34ft 1in Height: 12ft 6½in Wing area: 210 sq ft	Empty: 8,000lb Gross: 11,400lb	Max speed: 475 mph at 21,000ft Ceiling: 42,000ft Range: 564 miles at 240 mph	4×Hispano 20mm cannon; 2×1,000lb bombs or 4×300lb RP	
de Havilland Sea Hornet F.20	2×2,030 hp Rolls-Royce Merlin 133/134	Span: 45ft 0in Length: 36ft 8in Height: 14ft 2in Wing area: 361 sq ft	Gross: 18,250lb	Max speed: 431 mph at 10,000ft Ceiling: 35,000ft Range: 1,500 miles	4×20 mm cannon; 8×60lb RP or 2,000lb bombs	1
de Havilland Sea Hornet NF.21	2×2,030 hp Rolls-Royce Merlin 133/134	Span: 45ft 0in Length: 37ft 0in Height: 14ft 0in Wing area: 362 sq ft	Empty: 14,230lb Gross: 19,530lb	Max speed: 430 mph at 22,000ft Ceiling: 36,500ft Range: 1,500 miles	4×20 mm cannon; 8×60lb RP or 2×1,000lb bombs	2
Hawker Sea Fury FB.11	1×2,480 hp Bristol Centaurus 18	Span: 38ft 4¾in Length: 34ft 8in Height: 15ft 10½in Wing area: 280 sq ft	Empty: 9,240lb Gross: 12,500lb	Max speed: 460 mph at 18,000ft Ceiling: 35,800ft Range: 700 miles at 30,000ft	4×20mm cannon; 12×60lb RP or 2×1,000lb bombs	1
de Havilland Sea Vampire F.20	1×3,000lb st DH Goblin 2	Span: 38ft 0in Length: 30ft 9in Height: 8ft 10in Wing area: 266 sq ft	Gross: 12,660lb	Max speed: 526 mph Range: 1,145 miles at 350 mph and 30,000ft	4×20mm cannon	1
Gloster Meteor T.7	2×3,500lb st Rolls-Royce Derwent 8	Span: 37ft 2in Length: 43ft 6in Height: 13ft 0in Wing area: 350 sq ft	Empty: 10,645lb Gross: 14,230lb	Max speed: 590 mph at 10,000ft Ceiling: 45,000ft Range —	—	2
Hiller HTE-2	1×200 hp Franklin 6V4-200	Rotor dia: 35ft 0in Length: 28ft 6in Height: 9ft 6in	Empty: 1,656lb Gross: 2,500lb	Max speed: 84 mph Cruising: 70 mph Range: 135 miles	—	2
Hunting Percival Sea Prince	2×550 hp Alvis Leonides 125	Span: 56ft 0in Length: 46ft 4in Height: 16ft 1in Wing area: 365 sq ft	Empty: 8,850lb Gross: 11,850lb	Max speed: 223 mph at 2,000ft Cruising: 183 mph Ceiling: 22,000ft Range: 400 miles	—	2
Short Sturgeon TT.2	2×1,660 hp Rolls-Royce Merlin 140S	Span: 59ft 9in Length: 48ft 10½in Height: 13ft 2½in Wing area: 564 sq ft	Empty: 17,647lb Gross: 22,350lb	Max speed: 370 mph Ceiling: 32,900ft Range: 1,600 miles	—	2
Westland Dragonfly HR.3	1×550 hp Alvis Leonides 50	Rotor dia: 49ft Length: 57ft 6½in Height: 12ft 11in	Empty: 4,397lb Gross: 5,870lb	Max speed: 103 mph Cruising: 81 mph Ceiling: 13,500ft	—	2

Type	Powerplant	Dimensions	Weights	Performance	Armament	Crew
Supermarine Attacker F.1	1×5,100lb st Rolls-Royce Nene 3	Span: 36ft 11in Length: 37ft 6in Height: 9ft 11in Wing area: 226 sq ft	Empty: 8,434lb Gross: 11,500lb	Max speed: 590 mph at S/L Cruising: 355 mph Ceiling: 45,000ft Range: 590 miles	4×20mm cannon	1
Fairey Firefly AS.7	1×1,965 hp Rolls-Royce Griffon 59	Span: 44ft 6in Length: 38ft 3in Height: 13ft 3in Wing area: 342½ sq ft	Empty: 11,016lb Gross: 13,970lb	Max speed: 300 mph at 10,750ft Cruising: 275 mph Ceiling: 25,500ft Range: 860 miles at 166 mph	—	3
Westland Wyvern S.4	1×4,110 ehp Armstrong Siddeley Python ASP.3	Span: 44ft 0in Length: 42ft 3in Height: 15ft 9in Wing area: 355 sq ft	Empty: 15,608lb Gross: 24,500lb	Max speed: 383 mph at S/L Cruising: 343 mph at 20,000ft Ceiling: 28,000ft Range: 904 miles	4×20 mm cannon; 16×RP or 1×torpedo or 3×1,000lb bombs	1
Westland Whirlwind HAS.7	1×750 hp Alvis Leonides Major 755/1	Rotor dia: 54ft Length: 41ft 8½in Height: 15ft 4½in	Empty: 5,170lb Gross: 7,800lb	Max speed: 109½ mph at S/L Hover ceiling: 9,400ft Range: 334 miles at 86 mph	—	3
Boulton Paul Sea Balliol T.21	1×1,280 hp Rolls-Royce Merlin 35	Span: 39ft 4in Length: 35ft 1½in	Gross: 8,410lb	Max speed: 288 mph Ceiling: 32,500ft	—	2
Short SB.6 Seamew	1×Armstrong Siddeley Mamba	Span: 55ft 0in Length: 41ft 0in	Empty: 9,795lb Gross: 15,000lb	Max speed: 235 mph Range: 750 miles	—	2
Hawker Sea Hawk FGA.6	1×5,200lb st Rolls-Royce Nene 103	Span: 39ft 0in Length: 39ft 10in Height: 8ft 9in Wing area: 278 sq ft	Empty: 9,560lb Gross: 16,200lb	Max speed: 524 mph at 10,000ft Ceiling: 44,500ft Radius of action: 288 miles with 1,000lb of bombs	4×20 mm cannon; 10×RP; 2×500lb bombs or 100 gal drop tanks	1
Douglas Skyraider AEW.1	1×2,700 hp Wright Cyclone R-3350-26WA	Span: 50ft 0¼in Length: 38ft 10in Height: 15ft 8in Wing area: 400 sq ft	Empty: 13,614lb Gross: 24,000lb	Max speed: — Cruising: 250 mph Ceiling: 36,000ft Max range: 868 miles (internal fuel)	—	3
de Havilland Sea Devon C.20	2×340 hp DH Gipsy Queen 70	Span: 57ft 0in Length: 39ft 4in Height: 13ft 4in Wing area: 335 sq ft	Empty: 5,780lb Gross: 8,500lb	Max speed: 210 mph Cruising: 179 mph Ceiling: 20,000ft Range: 1,000 miles	—	8 seats
de Havilland Sea Heron C.20	4×250 hp DH Gipsy Queen 30	Span: 71ft 6in Length: 48ft 6in Height: 15ft 7in Wing area: 499 sq ft	Empty: 8,150lb Gross: 13,500lb	Max speed: 183 mph Ceiling: 18,500ft Range: 915 miles	—	—
Hawker Hunter T.8	1×7,550lb st Rolls-Royce Avon 122	Span: 33ft 8in Length: 48ft 10½in Height: 13ft 2in Wing area: 349 sq ft	Empty: 13,360lb Gross: 17,200lb	Max speed: Mach 0.92 at 36,000ft Ceiling: 47,000ft	1×20mm Aden cannon; various u/w stores	2
Hawker Hunter GA.11	1×7,500lb st Rolls-Royce Avon 113	Span: 33ft 8in Length: 45ft 10½in Height: 13ft 2in Wing area: 340 sq ft	Empty: 12,543lb Gross: 17,100lb	Max speed: Mach 0.94 at 36,000ft Ceiling: 50,000ft	various u/w stores	1
de Havilland Sea Venom FAW.22	1×5,300lb st DH Ghost 105	Span: 42ft 10in Length: 36ft 8in Height: 8ft 6¼in Wing area: 280 sq ft	Gross: 15,800lb	Max speed: 575 mph at S/L Ceiling: 40,000ft Range: 705 miles	4×20mm cannon; 8×60lb RP or bombs	2
Fairey Gannet AS.4	1×3,035 ehp Armstrong Siddeley Double Mamba 101	Span: 54ft 4in Length: 43ft 0in Height: 13ft 8½in	Empty: 15,069lb Gross: 19,600lb	Max speed: 299 mph Cruising: 150 mph Ceiling: 25,000ft Range: 662 miles	Provision for 2× homing torpedoes, mines or depth charges	3

Type	Powerplant	Dimensions	Weights	Performance	Armament	Crew
Supermarine Scimitar F.1	2×11,250lb st Rolls-Royce Avon 202	Span: 37ft 2in Length: 55ft 4in Height: 15ft 3in	Gross: 40,000lb	Max speed: 710 mph at 10,000ft	4×Aden cannon; 4×Sidewinder AAM or 12×RP or 4×1,000lb bombs	1
Armstrong Whitworth Meteor TT.20	2×Rolls-Royce Derwent	Span: 43ft 0in Length: 48ft 6in Height: 13ft 11in Wing area: 374 sq ft	Empty: 12,019lb Gross: 16,542lb	Max speed: 554 mph at 10,000ft Ceiling: 40,000ft	—	2
de Havilland Sea Vixen FAW.1	2×11,230lb st Rolls-Royce Avon 208	Span: 51ft 0in Length: 55ft 7in Height: 10ft 9in Wing area: 648 sq ft	Gross: 35,000lb	Max speed: 645 mph at 10,000ft Ceiling: 48,000ft	4×Firestreak AAM; 28×2in RP or 2×1,000lb bombs	2
Fairey Gannet AEW.3	1×3,875 ehp Armstrong Siddeley Double Mamba 102	Span: 54ft 4in Length: 44ft 0in Height: 16ft 10in	Gross: 25,000lb	Max speed: 250 mph Cruising: 130/140 mph Ceiling: 25,000ft Endurance: 5/6hr	None	2
Blackburn Buccaneer S.1	2×7,100lb st DH Gyron Junior	Span: 44ft 0in Length: 63ft 5in Height: 16ft 3in Wing area: 515 sq ft	Gross: 45,000lb	Max speed: 720 mph at S/L	up to 8,000lb bombs (4,000lb internal)	2
Westland Wessex HAS.1	1×1,450 shp Napier Gazelle 160	Rotor dia: 56ft 0in Length: 65ft 10in Height: 15ft 10in	Gross: 12,600lb	Max speed: 138 mph Range: 340 miles	2×a/s homing torpedoes	4
Westland Wessex HU.5	2×1,350 shp coupled Bristol Siddeley Gnome 110/111	Rotor dia: 56ft 0in Length: 48ft 4½in Height: 16ft 2in	Empty: 8,657lb Gross: 13,500lb	Max speed: 132 mph at S/L Hover ceiling: 5,500ft Range: 270 miles	variety of small arms/SS.11 ASMs	1/3
Hiller HT.2	1×305 hp Lycoming VO-540-A1B	Rotor dia: 35ft 4¾in Length: 28ft 6in Height: 9ft 3½in	Empty: 1,755lb Gross: 2,800lb	Max speed: 96 mph Cruising: 90 mph Hover ceiling: 5,800ft Range: 225 miles at S/L	—	2
Hawker Siddeley Sea Vixen FAW.2	2×11,230lb st Rolls-Royce Avon 208	Span: 51ft 0in Length: 55ft 7in Height: 10ft 9in Wing area: 648 sq ft	Gross: 37,000lb	Max speed: 640 mph Ceiling: 48,000ft	4×Red Top AAM; 2×retractable pods with 14×2in RP; 4×500lb bombs	2
Westland Wasp	1×710 shp Rolls-Royce Nimbus 103 or 104	Rotor dia: 32ft 3in Length: 40ft 4in Height: 11ft 10in	Empty: 3,418lb Gross: 5,500lb	Max speed: 120 mph at S/L Ceiling: 12,500ft Range: 270 miles at 110 mph	2×Mk 44 torpedoes or depth charges or 2×AS.12 ASMs	2
Hawker Siddeley Buccaneer S.2	2×11,100lb st Rolls-Royce Spey 101	Span: 44ft 0in Length: 63ft 5in Height: 16ft 3in Wing area: 515 sq ft	Gross: 45,000lb	Max speed: Mach 0.85 at 200ft Range: 3,000 miles	up to 16,000lb mixed ordnance	2
McDonnell Douglas Phantom FG.1	2×12,250lb st Rolls-Royce Spey 201	Span: 38ft 5in Length: 57ft 7in Height: 16ft 1in Wing area: 530 sq ft	Empty: 30,000lb Gross: 56,000lb	Max speed: Mach 2.1 (1,386 mph) Ceiling: 70,000ft Combat radius: 500 miles	4×Sparrow AAM; 4×Sidewinder AAM; up to 10,000lb u/w stores	2
Westland Sea King HAS.2	2×1,660 shp Rolls-Royce Gnome H.1400	Rotor dia: 62ft 0in Length overall: 72ft 8in Fuselage length: 55ft 9¾in Height: 15ft 11in	Empty: 13,000lb Gross: 21,000lb	Cruising: 129 mph at S/L Hover ceiling: 5,000ft Range: 764 miles	4×Mk 46 a/s torpedoes or 4×Mk 11 depth charges	4
Westland/ Aérospatiale Gazelle HT.2	1×592 shp Turboméca Astazou	Rotor dia: 34ft 5½in Length overall: 39ft 3½in Fuselage length: 31ft 3½in	Empty: 2,022lb Gross: 3,970lb	Max speed: 164 mph at S/L Cruising: 144 mph Hover ceiling: 9,350ft Range: 416 miles	various rockets, ASMs	2